COMMON ARCHITECTURE

SUNWOO KIM

ORO EDITIONS

I have always wondered about the unique value of architecture, particularly as a form of knowledge rather than merely a practice. This inquiry stems from a fundamental challenge: I find it difficult to articulate why a building is considered "good architecture" or why a person is deemed a "good architect" within a logical and intellectually consistent framework.

This book represents my first attempt to address this question, both as someone who practices and studies architecture. Over the years, I have encountered many individuals who sought to define what constitutes good architecture. However, their explanations often fell short. Some reduced architecture to a practice concerned solely with designing buildings. Others elevated architects to a mythic status, portraying them as intellectual and creative individuals with comprehensive knowledge of society at large.

To me, these perspectives were either logically inconsistent or overly romanticized architecture and the role of architects. I must also admit, that I once equated awards and popularity with quality in architecture and architects. I rarely questioned why certain buildings or architects garnered accolades, instead simply admiring their celebrated designs, recognition, and, most significantly, their aesthetic appeal.

However, I had the opportunity to learn from Peter Eisenman, who taught me the importance of "reading" architecture rather than merely "seeing" it. By this, I mean that while architecture is undeniably a visual practice, architects must be trained to discern the intention and reasoning behind a design rather than focusing solely on its aesthetic outcome. When the intention behind a work and its resulting design are cohesive, we can evaluate a building within a fair and consistent value system. Conversely, when these elements are misaligned, it becomes challenging to discuss why a particular work of architecture is good or bad.

This lesson from Eisenman led me to question the allure of visually striking forms often featured in magazines. If I had believed that dazzling projects were the ultimate goal of architecture, such doubts might never have arisen. To illustrate this, consider cinema: while blockbuster films

FIGURE 1 Auditorio De Tenerife, SANTIAGO CALATRAVA

FIGURE 2 Port House Antwerp, ZAHA HADID

like *Avengers* are entertaining, they do not represent the common values of film as an art form, nor are they inherently better than works like *Parasite*. Blockbusters inevitably cater to market demands over disciplinary values, prioritizing mass appeal. Similarly, the glamorous designs of starchitects represent "blockbuster architecture," created for the wealthiest 0.1%, reflecting the priorities of the elite and their capital rather than the common value of architecture.

Even apart from capital, blockbuster architecture has another limitation: it often prioritizes iconicity—forms that are easily marketable. These designs inevitably align with market demand and branding strategies. Beneath the glossy surfaces of these projects lie the commodification of personal styles, often at the expense of the diversity and commonness of our shared environment.

This phenomenon raises further concerns beyond market dynamics. Many creative fields face a similar issue, where creators sacrifice individuality to align with client demands and trends. The relentless pursuit of novelty for market attention becomes hollow and oppressive.[1] However, this does not mean I outright reject market-driven architecture. As Winston Churchill famously said, "We shape our buildings, and afterwards, our buildings shape us." I believe architects must look beyond market demand to explore more fundamental, common values in architecture.

Without establishing common values, meaningful dialogue about any discipline becomes impossible. And without dialogue, there can be no debate about what is "good" or "bad." My hope is that this book serves as a starting point for such conversations.

1 Semper, "Science, Industry, and Art," p.139

CONTENTS

PROLOGUE

1 THE ROLE OF ARCHITECTURE AND ARCHITECTS 010

2 THE BEGINNING OF COMMON ARCHITECTURE: TYPES & EXAMPLES 016

3 COMMON MEDIA OF ARCHITECTURE: FORM & DRAWING 030

4 WHAT IS TYPE? 038

1

THE ROLE OF ARCHITECTURE AND ARCHITECTS

BEYOND NEWNESS: WHY COMMONNESS MATTERS

Present-day architects, in their visionary compulsion to invent new techniques, have neglected their obligation to be experts in existing conventions.[2]

ROBERT VENTURI

What could "common architecture" be? The thoughts that come to mind include "ordinary," "unobtrusive," and "rational," which, in some ways, can be seen as the opposite of "new."

So let me ask again: Does architecture need to be new? I dare to say that architecture is a field that does not necessarily need to pursue novelty. While other design and art fields inherently require new attempts, finding value in the newness itself, architecture is far too specialized to be considered just another art form.

The completion of a building requires much more than creative activity. It demands interpreting regulations, managing clients and consultants, and extensive collaboration to meet various functional requirements. In practice, architectural work leans toward "commonness" rather than "newness."

Even if we concede that ordinary and familiar things have no inherent merit, can they truly be considered bad? People tend to instinctively favor novelty, believing that anything new is inherently better. Words like "innovation" and "invention" carry overwhelmingly positive connotations, and it's rare to encounter someone who perceives them negatively.

In addressing this nearly universal preference for the new, the German philosopher Hegel offers a counterbalancing concept: Bad Infinity. I take this term as "consumptive perpetuity." According to Hegel, *Bad Infinity* refers to the denial of limits, a blind belief in the necessity and possibility of endlessly producing something new. In other words, the absence of perceived boundaries leads to an obsessive compulsion to create novelty.

Pier Vittorio Aureli extends this idea, arguing that such behavior ultimately amounts to consuming the new to create more of the new—essentially creating nothing. When architects reject established patterns or conventions in pursuit of originality alone, they risk imposing arbitrary decisions that can lead to chaos. In this chaos, the criteria for determining what is truly "new" dissolve, making it imperative to approach the value of novelty with greater criticality.

Humans have a cognitive limit in perceiving and processing "newness" or novel stimuli. Our perceptual abilities are more attuned to the gradual pace of change in everyday life. If architecture is fundamentally a discipline concerned with shaping the physical environment we inhabit, then it is reasonable to argue that architecture aligns more closely with the rhythms of ordinary life than with the pursuit of unrelenting newness.

> Today if I were to talk about architecture, I would say that it is a ritual rather than a creative process. I say this fully understanding the bitterness and the comfort of the ritual.[3]
>
> **ALDO ROSSI**

Architecture is a field where pursuing commonness is more rational than chasing novelty. Therefore, creating true innovation in architecture must be grounded in the commonness established by existing conventions and types. Without this foundation, creativity risks becoming merely an arbitrary experiment by the individual designer.[4]

WHAT IS ARCHITECTS' UNIQUE ROLE?

The task of architecture is to reify—that is, to transform into public, generic and thus graspable common things...[5]

PIER VITTORIO AURELI

Just like the title of this chapter, I have been pondering—and continue to ponder—what architects uniquely contribute to the built environment. At present, I can describe my role as designing buildings and coordinating with various consultants, including structural, civil, and MEP engineers, to ensure that projects are executed seamlessly and without complications. However, I find myself hesitant to claim that these responsibilities are the exclusive domain of architects. With adequate experience and research, general contractors can deliver well-functioning, aesthetically pleasing buildings that rival those designed by architects.

What, then, is the unique contribution that architects bring to the world? One of the most satisfying answers I have encountered comes from the oldest surviving text on architecture, *Ten Books on Architecture* by Vitruvius. In this book, Vitruvius emphasizes that if an architect cannot articulate their design in appropriate language, the architecture lacks the value necessary for meaningful engagement. Therefore, he argues that "writing" is one of the most crucial virtues of an architect. Vitruvius introduces this reasoning through the concepts of *Fabrica* and *Ratiocinatio*. *Fabrica* refers to the skills and actions involved in the physical construction of buildings, while *Ratiocinatio* denotes the intellectual activity that occurs during the conceptualization of a building. In essence, *Ratiocinatio* is the contemplation of "why" a building should exist in a specific way. Vitruvius argues that it is *Ratiocinatio* that is indispensable to architecture.[6] By distinguishing between construction and architecture,

Vitruvius captures the enduring tension between conception and execution, idea and reality, that has been inherent to the discipline since its inception. From as early as the Roman era, he recognized architecture as a field distinct from construction. He asserted that the unique role of the architect lies not in determining "what" or "how" to build, but in contemplating and articulating "why" a building should exist in the first place.

The second clue from Vitruvius regarding the unique role of architects lies in their distinct ability to perceive the world "through" the lens of architecture. While this may initially seem like an enigmatic statement, it underscores the philosophical and nuanced nature of architectural thinking—one that goes beyond merely explaining the reasoning behind designs. To illustrate what is meant by "looking at the world through architecture," we can consider the example of Vitruvius himself.

Vitruvius, a military engineer in the Roman Empire during the culmination of a century-long civil war, authored *The Ten Books on Architecture* as a tribute to Emperor Augustus. This period marked the advent of *Pax Romana*, a time of relative peace and stability. Through his treatise, Vitruvius sought to present a comprehensive framework for architecture that would provide intellectual and cultural legitimacy to the newly unified empire.[7]

One could argue that Vitruvius aimed to establish a standard for controlling the empire through architecture. However, architecture historian Indra Kagis McEwen offers a more nuanced and compelling interpretation of Vitruvius's intentions. In her book *Vitruvius: Writing the Body of Architecture*, McEwen suggests that the spirit of a unified empire could only be expressed through a consistent and exhaustive rationale of architecture, one that permeates the entire civic environment. This, she argues, is how Vitruvius envisioned the new world: as an undivided and pacified empire represented through comprehensive architectural logic rather than isolated monuments. In this view, the symbolism of the empire evolves into a form of knowledge embedded in its architectural framework.

This interpretation highlights a more profound role for architecture and architects who see the world "through" architecture. To summarize, the construction of architectural logic holds greater significance than the mere construction of buildings. If architecture is understood as a type of philosophy, architects may not always have the liberty to choose the problems they address. However, they do possess the freedom to translate their philosophical insights into architectural logic. It is this foundational emphasis on logic, rather than design alone, that architects should prioritize.

I should explain exactly whom I mean by an architect; for it is no carpenter that I would have you compare to the greatest exponents of other disciplines: the carpenter is but an instrument in the hands of the architect. Him I consider the architect, who by sure and wonderful reason and method, knows both how to devise through his own mind and energy, and to realize by construction, whatever can be most beautifully fitted out of the noble needs of people, by the movement of weights and the joining and massing of bodies.[8]

LEON BATTISTA ALBERTI

2 Venturi, "Complexity and Contradiction in Architecture," p.43

3 Rossi, "A Scientific Autobiography," p.37

4 de Quincy, "Invention, in Historical Dictionary," p.179-83 (p.181)

5 Aureli, "The Possibility of Absolute Architecture," p41-42

6 McEwen, "Vitruvius: Writing the Body of Architecture," p.32-33

7 Refer to Pier Vittorio Aureli's AA School Lecture: "Theory and Ethos: Towards a Common Architectural Language" Part 1 (2012)

8 Alberti, "Ten Books on the Art of Construction," p.31

2
THE BEGINNING OF COMMON ARCHITECTURE: TYPES AND EXAMPLES

> However, the putting forward of a formal language is not enough in itself, since any means of communication must have a recognizable order, either inherent or imposed...It will be seen that systems provide a discipline rather than a limit to this process. Systems deny only the arbitrary, the picturesque and the romantic: the subjective and personal interpretation of the order.[9]
>
> **PETER EISENMAN**

Why, then, are logic and communication crucial in architecture? The importance of communication is evident in Vitruvius's assertion that "if one cannot explain the work, it is not architecture." Even if we concede that something unexplainable might still qualify as architecture, I believe it cannot be considered good architecture. The inability to logically explain one's architecture often reflects an over-reliance on personal taste during the design process.

Taste, by its nature, is subjective. When one attempts to communicate personal preferences to others, there is often a degree of ambiguity that makes comprehension challenging. While shared tastes make understanding easier, differing tastes leave little room for persuasion; it simply becomes a matter of disagreement. A prime example of "architecture driven by taste" is particularly evident in the works of some starchitects.

As their fame grows, the market increasingly demands their distinctive style rather than their critical reasoning. Architects with strong stylistic gestures exemplify this trend. For those who admire a particular architect's style, their designs are celebrated. However, the same style can alienate others, who reject the work for precisely the same reason.

Alan Colquhoun addressed this issue by arguing that designs rooted in intuition and taste cannot adequately address the diverse and complex demands of contemporary society. Instead, architects must adopt an analytical and systematic thought process to develop their ideas and effectively communicate their designs. This approach not only enhances the clarity of architectural expression but also ensures that architecture remains relevant and meaningful within a broader social and cultural context.[10] This effectively highlights the limitations of design driven by "taste" and architecture that cannot be explained.

What, then, is architecture that communicates? Alberti draws a comparison between architecture and rhetoric—the art of persuasion. He argues that an architect, like a rhetorician, must communicate intentions clearly and persuasively by logically composing architectural elements, much like constructing sentences in a language.[11] The most significant distinction between architecture and other forms of communication is that architecture's logic is communicated not to a specific audience but to all members of a city, making its impact broader and more encompassing. This relationship between architecture, rhetoric, and communication is encapsulated in the concept of *Concinnitas* introduced by Alberti in his treatise *De re Aedificatoria*. Roughly translated, *Concinnitas* means "beauty" and "harmony" in Latin. Pier Vittorio Aureli elaborates that, for Alberti, beauty is not merely a visual quality but "something that enables communication." Extending this logic further, *the raison d'être* of beauty in architecture lies in its capacity to convey intentions and ideas through the logical arrangement of architectural elements.[12]

Another anecdote about Alberti's work is that he wrote *De re Aedificatoria* in Latin. At the time, Latin was the language of the highly educated elite—nobles and clergy—and books themselves were luxury items accessible only to these privileged classes before the advent of printing. This suggests that Alberti did not write his treatise for architects but rather for the ruling class.

Why was *Concinnitas*—symbolizing harmony and communication—so important to the ruling class during the Renaissance? Families like the Medici, emblematic of the era's aristocracy, often amassed their wealth through corruption or financial schemes. This created numerous political and economic issues, and Alberti recognized the need to justify such wealth.[13]

In this context, the building façade became a crucial medium for communicating and legitimizing the wealth of ruling class to the public. Alberti's façade design principles provided a logical framework for representing aristocratic wealth as a public good, integrating these private structures into the broader urban environment. By using their buildings as urban devices for public betterment, the aristocracy sought to rationalize their wealth and communicate this justification to all citizens.[14] This highlights that *Concinnitas* in architecture extends beyond aesthetic beauty—it encompasses the strategic communication of social and political intentions.

As demonstrated, in architecture, communication is more critical than visual appeal. "Good" architecture supports communication through a consistent logical system, rather than relying on striking Instagram-worthy images. Architects must prioritize the logic and communicative potential of their designs, ensuring their architecture serves as a medium for meaningful dialogue.

9 Eisenman, "The Formal Basis of Modern Architecture," p.21

10 Colquhoun, "Typology and Design Method," Perspecta 12 (1969), p.71

11 Refer to Pier Vittorio Aureli's AA School Lecture: "Theory and Ethos: Towards a Common Architectural Language" Part 2 (2012)

12 Refer to the same lecture above

13 Refer to the same lecture above

14 Refer to the same lecture above

FIGURE 3 Palazzo Rucellai, ALBERTI

WHAT IS COMMON IS EASIER TO COMMUNICATE

> An effective communication...requires legibility and reciprocated intellection, which depend on a shared knowledge and language, in short: conventions.[15]
>
> **SAM JACOBY**

Earlier, I mentioned that good architecture can achieve effective communication through consistent logic. Now, we must consider what kind of logic is most suited for communication. While consistency is important, excessively esoteric logic can hinder understanding. For example, in religion, phenomena like extremism or sectarianism arise from the absence of a "common" logic. This illustrates that not only is consistent logic crucial, but the type of logic is equally significant.

I believe that common logic is most suitable for communication and serves as a strong starting point for good architecture. But what constitutes common logic in architecture? First, it must be familiar to us and intuitively understood within a cultural context without requiring elaborate explanation. Architecture inherently involves historical, functional, and technical interpretations, and these interpretations must be organized into a universally accessible framework. This is where convention comes into play.

Quatremère de Quincy emphasized the value of convention, stating that "Conventions enable the artist to give to every passion its proper language, to every condition, to every age its habits, manners, and mode of speech."[16] Conventions hold rational logic while embodying the sensibilities of a particular era or culture, providing a healthy benchmark for creative endeavors.

Thus, conventions can be regarded as a representative common logic for good architecture. They allow us to balance rationality with cultural and historical resonance, making them an ideal foundation for creating meaningful, communicative, and enduring architectural works.

In the discussion above, I described convention as a "benchmark for creative endeavors." If we interpret this only in visual terms, it's easy to dismiss convention as outdated or conservative. However, Peter Carl argues the opposite: convention is, in fact, the prerequisite for freedom.[17]

This perspective reveals an intriguing tension between creativity and convention. According to Peter Carl's reasoning, familiarity with convention doesn't lead to staleness but rather equips creators with the confidence to handle conventions skillfully and generate something new.

Furthermore, novelty born from convention or commonness is not "radical" or "novelty for the sake of novelty." Instead, it is "systematic novelty" rooted in a deep understanding and respect for commonness. This kind of novelty supports more meaningful creative processes, as it balances innovation with conventions.

15 Jacoby, "The Reasoning of Architecture: Type and The Problem of HIstoricity," (2013) p.3

16 de Quincy, "Essay on Imitation," p.62

17 Carl, "Type, Field, Culture, Praxis," Architectural Design Architectural Urbanism 209, p.40
"What is common-to-all exerts a claim upon freedom; freedom dependscupon what is common-to-all for its meaning (freedom would otherwise be alienation)."

COMMUNICATION STRATEGY OF CLASSICAL ARCHITECTURE

Language serves as both a medium for facilitating communication among people and as a part of, or even a reflection of, societal structure itself. As civilization culture evolved, particularly in the Western context, architecture began to transcend its role as mere physical construction, acquiring diverse meanings. This shift became prominent during the Renaissance, when theories and writings emerged that treated architecture as a "language" for conveying social and political ideas. Consequently, architecture established itself as a significant socio-political discipline.

The cornerstone of viewing architecture as a language lies in the system of orders formalized by Vitruvius. These orders functioned like words in architectural composition, communicating clear meanings. For instance, the Doric order, symbolizing masculinity, is the simplest and least adorned, typically placed at the base of a structure. The Ionic order, representing femininity, is more ornate and is positioned higher on buildings.

These classical architectural elements existed within a clearly defined symbolic system, making their "grammar" absolute. This absoluteness ensured that these classical elements could be universally applied with consistent logic, much like language.

While classical architectural design adhered to this common grammar, architects skillfully manipulated these elements within its boundaries to achieve both commonness and novelty. This duality allowed classical architecture to maintain its timeless appeal while fostering creativity within a shared framework.

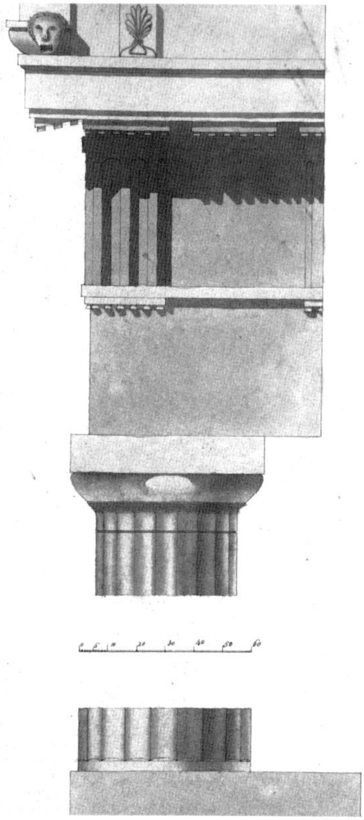

FIGURE 4 Doric Order (Left), Ionic Order (Right)

FIGURE 5 In the design of the colonnades at St. Peter's Basilica, Bernini intentionally combined the simplest Doric columns with the more intricate Ionic entablature to improve constructability. This deliberate departure from traditional pairings exemplifies an "intentional mistake" made possible by the universal and consistent logic of classical architectural grammar.

WHAT IS THE COMMON LANGUAGE OF CONTEMPORARY ARCHITECTURE?

TYPES

Types—the materials with which the architect works—are seen to be colored by ideology and assume meaning within the structural framework in which architecture is produced. In accepting a type, or in rejecting it, the architect is thus entering into the realm of communication in which the life of the individual man is involved with that of society...if a work of architecture needs the type to establish a path for its communication—to avoid the gap between the past, the moment of creation, and the world in which the architecture is ultimately placed—then types must be the the starting point of the design process.[18]

RAFAEL MONEO

Classical architecture was built upon the Vitruvian legacy, which relied on a representation system of orders. However, as society became increasingly complex—particularly with the rise of the economy as the central ethos—this legacy began to lose relevance. While this shift arguably began in the 16th century, it became unmistakable following the French Revolution, rendering Vitruvian principles obsolete. The decline of this legacy inevitably spurred efforts to establish a new architectural convention or language suitable for a society shaped by a burgeoning bourgeois class. One prominent candidate for this new convention was the concept of type.

The term type originates from the Greek *typos*, meaning "matrix," "mold," or "original form," and the Latin *typus*, meaning "figure," "image," "form," or "kind." Collectively, these origins suggest that type refers to a formal structure or a category that encompasses multiple forms. In this sense, any action to group things by common characteristics, or the shared features themselves, can be understood as type.

In architecture, how is type understood? The most common approach is classification based on building function, such as hospital type or school type. However, strictly speaking, these are not types but rather nomenclature—convenient naming systems used for descriptive purposes. By contrast, terms such as "courtyard," "row house," or "palazzo" align more closely with the concept of type because they represent formal structures.

As Aldo Rossi eloquently articulated in his book *The Architecture of the City*, a building can adopt various functions throughout its history while preserving its formal structure. In architecture, form holds greater permanence than function, making it a more common and essential value. Just as language communicates through written characters, an architect's intent is conveyed through form. This permanence of form underscores its role as essence of common architecture, solidifying type as a key concept for commonncss.

Another reason type is a key concept in common architecture lies in the information it embodies. Among the various forms and structures that have appeared repeatedly throughout history, only some are recognized as types. This selection highlights the importance of understanding why certain forms are accepted as types, emphasizing their capacity to convey enduring cultural, functional, or symbolic significance. For instance, while European history features numerous forms of housing, only a few—such as row houses, palazzos, and apartments—have become types. These types transcend mere formal structures or stylistic choices; they represent accumulated sets of knowledge that convey subtle nuances of political and economic context.

Take, for example, the courtyard houses in Siena. This type emerged from a unique set of political and legal conditions designed to regulate the city. In particular, restrictions on the buildings prohibited architectural additions displaying wealth or political power toward street, redirecting such expressions to the interior spaces of houses. This regulation led to the development of courtyard house type, a natural resultant of the socio-political dynamics of its time.[19] This indicates that types are not merely widespread forms; rather, they are the product of a cohesive relationship between formal structure and political/economic implications. Without this relationship, they would be reduced to mere images or diagrams.[20] This is why Rafael Moneo stated that "type is un-representable."

In conclusion, type is not merely a design tool, like a diagram, but a comprehensive and complex system of information embedded with the history and experiences of a given culture. This inclusivity and complexity elevate type to a fundamental element of common architecture.

The final reason type is not only valuable for common architecture but also for commonness in general lies in its meaning. When we refer to objects, buildings, or phenomena as types, it inherently suggests that they have become widespread and normalized. For example, during the COVID-19 pandemic, individuals wearing masks became a type of normal citizen, whereas masks previously carried several negative connotations.

Thus, for something to become a type, it must be based on its universality—it must be common to all. Conversely, uncommon things cannot be identified as types. This inseparable link between type and commonness provides architects with a valid and reliable starting point for design.

EXAMPLES

As an architect I try to be guided not by habit but by a conscious sense of the past—by precedent, thoughtfully considered...An architect should use convention and make it vivid. I mean he should use convention unconventionally.[21]

ROBERT VENTURI

Architectural design, by its nature, relies heavily on a multitude of examples. Consequently, architects often question whether their ideas are truly original or derived, perhaps unconsciously, from prior examples. In this sense, architectural design exists in a tension between examples from the past and the experiences of the present. As the well-known axiom states, "There is nothing new under the sun," making it inevitable for designers to draw upon examples. This "example approach" is perhaps the most common framework for lending authority, historicity, and validity to a work.

Unlike types, however, examples are neither general nor comprehensive; they are particular and specific. Examples are chosen precisely because they clarify an idea in the clearest way possible—rarely to introduce ambiguity. Furthermore, examples are real, concrete instances that have already demonstrated their utility and value. In this way, examples complement type by providing concreteness to its generality.

While I do not claim that the interplay between type and example is valid in every aspect of design, I argue that this complementarity encourages architects to respect history and conventions before prioritizing creativity. This respect is essential for constructing a communicative framework rooted in common logic, which is, ultimately, the goal of common architecture.

18 Moneo, "On Typology," Oppositions 13 (1978), p.37

19 Sheherazade, "Street as a Project," Chapter 2, TU Delft Ph.D Thesis

20 Vidler, "Third Typology," Oppositions Reader 1973-1984, p.15

21 Venturi, "Complexity and Contradiction in Architecture," p.42

3
COMMON MEDIA OF ARCHITECTURE: FORM & DRAWING

ETYMOLOGY OF "FORM"

Architecture is in essence the giving of form (itself an element) to intent, function, structure and techniques. Thus form is raised to be a position of primacy in the hierarchy of elements.[22]

PETER EISENMAN

Now, let us delve deeper into how the value of commonness can be interpreted within the discipline of architecture. Suppose I present a particular building as a good example of common architecture. To persuade others, it is only logical to explain the reasons using an objective medium. In architecture, form is the most appropriate concept for such communication, as it serves as a clear and objective medium for expressing ideas.

While there are other mediums for interpreting architecture, such as materials, construction quality, and spatial experience, these often fall short of being consistently objective. Materials and construction quality, for instance, depend heavily on the budget, not just the architect's skill. Even the most meticulous architect cannot ensure perfect construction quality if the client lacks the resources to hire skilled contractors. Similarly, spatial experience is inherently intangible, making it difficult to quantify or analyze objectively. Personal experiences often influence perceptions of space—positive for some and negative for others, depending on memories or emotions tied to that space.

In contrast, form is tangible and measurable. It exists as a physical reality that can be analyzed and understood equally by everyone. Because of this, form is exceptionally well-suited as an objective medium for communicating and analyzing the common values of architecture. It transcends subjective biases, enabling clear and logical dialogue about architectural intent and quality.

This perspective might seem to oversimplify the diverse values of architecture, but the term "form" gains additional significance when we examine its etymology. Derived from the Latin *forma*, the word traces back to two Greek terms with distinct meanings: *eidos and morphe. Eidos* refers to a "conceptual" form, emphasizing the idea or principle behind something, and serves as the root of the word "idea." In contrast, morphe denotes the "visual" form, focusing on the physical appearance that we can perceive.[23]

This distinction highlights a tension between two approaches: one that centers on the visible and tangible as the core of human experience, and another that prioritizes the principles and logic underlying visible phenomena. Neither the visible nor the logic is inherently superior; instead, the process of translating an architect's reasoning and intentions into visible form is what matters most. This tension between conceptual and physical forms is at the heart of common architecture.

Thus, form is not merely a tool for quantifying and framing a building within objective criteria. It also encompasses the process of understanding and representing the principles and logic of design. This multifaceted value of form plays a central role in making architecture communicable in an objective and common manner.

22 Eisenman, "Formal Basis of Modern Architecture," p.33
23 Aureli, "The Possibility of Absolute Architecture," p.30

RECORD OF FORM: "DRAWINGS"

[B]oth the form and the proportion would need to manifest themselves in the most evident way, and the eye would need to be able to grasp their relations with the greatest accuracy; and this would require all of them to present themselves in a single vertical plane: a thing that never happens and never can happen.[24]

JEAN-NICOLAS-LOUIS DURAND

We are exploring the "common media" for expressing and analyzing architecture, and the previous discussion established why form is particularly suitable for this purpose. If form is akin to language, it requires a system of writing—symbols that must be universally applicable. Jean-Nicolas-Louis Durand's insight above precisely addresses the challenges of recording form while proposing the most effective method: the orthogonal projection. But why is this method the most accurate for representing form?

To understand, let us compare orthogonal projection with perspective drawing. Perspective was developed to depict objects "as they appear" to the eye. However, perspective introduces distortions: objects appear longer or shorter depending on their distance from the vanishing point. Consequently, the presentation of perspective drawings varies with the viewer's position.

In contrast, orthogonal projection represents forms at a fixed scale, unaffected by the viewer's position. Paradoxically, while this method assumes an impossible vantage point—one that does not exist in real life—it provides the most accurate and distortion-free means of communication. This precision makes orthogonal projection ideal for collaboration and documentation in architecture.

FIGURE 6 Illustration Showing Principles Of Perspective

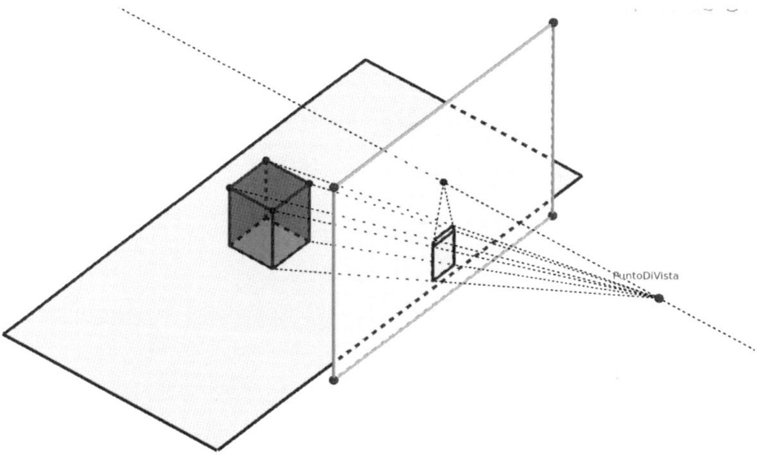

FIGURE 7 Illustration Showing Principles Of Perspective

24 Durand, "Precis of the Lecture on Architecture: With, Graphic Portion of the Lectures on Architecture," p.138

PLAN: THE MOST PIVOTAL DRAWING

Architectural drawings include the plan, which shows the layout of each floor; the section, which reveals vertical organization of the building; and the elevation, which displays the building's exterior. While each type of drawing serves a critical role, the plan holds particular significance, as expressed by Le Corbusier's famous statement, "The plan is the generator." But why is the plan considered more valuable than other drawings in architecture?

The concept and definition of the plan can be traced back to Vitruvius, who introduced *ichnographia* as one of the three methods of representing a building. The term *ichnographia* originates from the Greek words *ichnos* (meaning "footprint") and *graphe* (meaning "drawing"), referring to a plan that records the "footprint" or "trace" of a building.

As suggested by its etymological roots—implying "footprint" or "trace"—a plan is not merely a representation of a building's physical construction. It also signifies the conception of the building as envisioned in the architect's mind, independent of whether the structure has been built.[25] In this sense, the plan embodies the very essence of the architect's idea, offering a foundational glimpse into the spatial and functional intentions behind the design. Humans ultimately navigate the world on the ground, making the plan the most effective drawing for illustrating not only the horizontal organization of a building but also the architect's intentions.

The earliest recorded plan in history dates back to the Neolithic Natufian culture. Interestingly, this coincides with the period when humanity first transitioned to an agricultural lifestyle.[26] This overlap suggests a profound connection between the advent of settled living and the emergence of architectural planning, as the shift to farming likely necessitated more permanent and organized spatial planning. This shift naturally led to the emergence of more structured lifestyles, prompting people to plan spaces that accommodated their needs. As the shared term "plan" in English for both "the act of planning" and "floor plan" suggests, a plan is inherently tied to the act of organizing and translating human life patterns into physical presentations.

In essence, the plan allows us to design ways of living, while simultaneously providing a physical framework that shapes those lifestyles. For instance, naming spatial configurations like "centralized," "double-loaded corridor," or "courtyard" as types visible in floor plans is no coincidence. These types reflect the reciprocal relationship between planning and living, with the plan serving as a fundamental medium that bridges human intention and built form.

Within the "example approach," the plan has also proven to be an essential medium for communicating concepts effectively. For instance, works like Giovanni Battista Piranesi's Campo Marzio or Aldo Rossi's Città Analoga clearly articulate their ideas by collaging examples in plan format. Figure 8 depicts Piranesi's Campo Marzio plan, which is not a construction drawing but a conceptual drawing meant to convey his city planning intent. For Piranesi, Rome needed to be planned around its significant historical monuments, with functional considerations being secondary. This plan compresses centuries of historical monuments into a single drawing, clearly representing the logic he used to reimagine Rome.

In stark contrast to the functional zoning commonly used in modern urban planning, Piranesi approached the city as an organic assembly of historical examples. He articulated this idea in the poetic form of the Campo Marzio plan. Without the comprehensive nature of the plan, which allows the entire concept to be understood at a glance, effectively communicating such ideas would have been extremely difficult. Similarly, without referencing actual historical monuments as examples, Piranesi would not have been able to convey his intentions with such clarity.

As we have seen, a plan is not merely a drawing that depicts a horizontal slice of a building's floor. Instead, it represents the very process of concep-

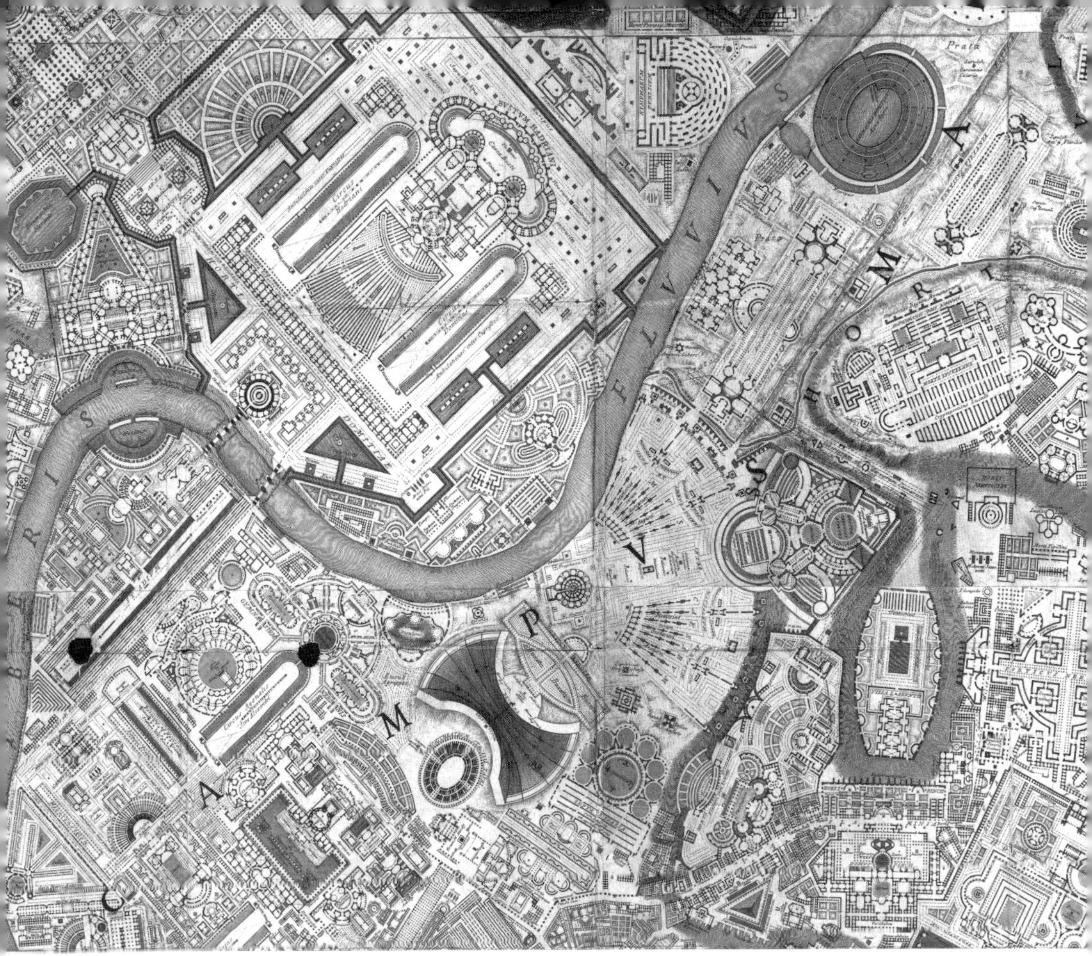

FIGURE 8 CAMPO MARZIO, Piranesi

tualizing a plan and translating it into physical form. Thus, the plan serves as an objective and common medium for effectively communicating an architect's intentions within the discipline of architecture.

25 Celedon, "Footprints," p.70
26 Aureli, "Life, Abstracted: Notes on the Floor Plan," p.3

4
WHAT IS TYPE?

FROM TAXONOMY TO TYPOLOGY

Up to this point, the book has provided a brief summary and introduction to its three main themes: 1. The reason why I pursue common architecture; 2. The architectural concepts most suitable for common architecture, namely "type" and "example"; 3. The media for objectively representing and analyzing type and example, "form" and "drawing." From now on, the discussion will delve into the architectural value of type and example in depth.

First, let us examine the historical background that gave rise to the concept of type. Starting in the mid-17th century, several centuries after the invention of the printing, doubts began to emerge about the classical architectural language of Vitruvius. This skepticism arose because the proportional systems of classical architecture, which were thought to be absolute, were found to exhibit a wide variety of forms from various treatises.

Claude Perrault, solidified these doubts in his book *Ordonnance*. In this work, he presented examples of how the proportional systems of classical architecture had been visually altered according to culture, region, and context. This led Perrault to argue that the notion of a priori and absolute "beauty" could not exist. Instead, he proposed that beauty is a relative concept, shaped by customs and culture.[27]

This crisis of classical architecture coincided with the rise of natural science and Enlightenment ethos in 17th- and 18th-century Europe. This intellectual movement brought about a significant shift in the way knowledge was perceived. Consequently, absolute knowledge reliant on transcendental metaphysics, such as religion, gradually lost its credibility, and logic and factual reasoning grounded in empirical analysis began to take its place.

In other words, this period marked the beginning of the widespread adoption of what we now call "scientific" thinking. One of the phenomena that epitomized this transformation was the emergence of taxonomy, a discipline essential for compiling encyclopedias, which aimed to systematically document all knowledge and objects in the world.

What is the first step in classification? It is to identify the essential characteristics of distinct objects. For instance, classifying living beings as "mammals," "reptiles," or "birds" requires an understanding of behavioral patterns or physical traits unique to each "species." Here, it is worth noting that the word species derives from the Latin word *specio*, meaning "to look at."

This implies that identifying and classifying the core of an object or phenomenon fundamentally relies on its visual attributes.[28] In architecture, taxonomy was understood as the act of categorizing past examples based on their essential forms or functions. These classified examples served as foundational materials and resources for rational architectural design. The book, *Cours D'architecture Qui Comprend Les Ordres De Vignole* by Augustin-Charles d'Aviler exemplifies this shift. In his work, d'Aviler analyzes the forms of historical examples and argues that combining these forms appropriately represents a rational design methodology suited to the needs of a new society.[29]

However, about thirty years later, criticisms of this approach began to emerge. The main argument was that rationalism, rooted in scientific and empirical analysis, reduced creative activities in the arts, including architecture, to the mechanical combination of forms and shapes from historical examples. In response to such criticism, Pierre Nativelle, proposed a method in his book *Nouveau Traité D'architecture* that maintained the rationalist approach while enabling innovation. He argued that classical architectural design typically followed a bottom-up process, where small architectural elements, such as a type of order, were selected first and then applied to the overall design. This approach, according to Nativelle, was more prone to mechanical combinations of examples due to their specificities.

To escape this, Nativelle suggested a top-down process in which the overall composition of buildings is analyzed first, and the smaller elements are designed subsequently.[30] The essence of his argument was to move away from being constrained by the minute details of examples and instead focus on the overall composition and structure of buildings. This approach, which could be considered abstract/diagrammatic, allowed creative activities within rationalism to transcend the mechanical combination of examples.

This shift naturally had a significant impact on many creative disciplines, and in architecture, it meant that visible appearances alone were no longer treated as the primary characteristics for classification. It was in this long-standing tension between the "visible" and the "invisible" that Quatremère de Quincy introduced the concept of type, bringing a resolution to this debate.

Starting in the next chapter, we will examine how the concept of type evolved in architecture, focusing on several key figures, beginning with Quatremère de Quincy.

27 Perrault, "Ordonnance des cinq especes de colonnes selon la method des anciens" (1683). 'Preface,' in Ordonnance, trans. By McEwen, with introduction by Alberto Perez-Gomez (1993), p.52

28 Celedon, "The Plan as Eidos," p.3

29 Jacoby, "The Reasoning of Architecture," p.37

30 Ibid., p.37

QUATREMERE DE QUINCY, "TYPE IS A PRIORI"

Type, by embodying the common-to-all, the underlying deep structure and generative principle but also the particularity of its possible forms, synthesizes the ideal and the real, reconceptualizing and eventually re-materializing the real through the ideal by considering the external image of resemblance as an internal idea that is limited.[31]

QUATREMERE DE QUINCY

In developing a new classification system to address the excessive reliance of taxonomy based on "visibility," Quatremère de Quincy naturally began questioning the origins of art and architecture. To classify something, one must grasp its essence, and to understand its essence, one must delve into its origins. Traditionally, the origins of art and architecture were believed to lie in nature, with imitation considered the means to achieve beauty. However, de Quincy redefined the concept of "imitation" to align with the rationalist analysis of his era.

For him, imitation was not the act of reproducing predetermined "images" or "principles" of nature but a process of universalizing and generalizing nature in a way that could be accepted by a given society and culture.[32] This suggests that beauty is not a preordained concept dictated by visual principles like proportion but a relative notion derived from analyzing common principles within phenomena and objects. This interpretation marks a significant departure from classical aesthetics. Similarly, the British painter Joshua Reynolds rejected "individuality" and advocated for "generalization" as a path to common truth and beauty.[33]

For de Quincy, type embodied this process of analyzing common principles and represented universality itself, thereby connecting it to the origins of art in beauty. He expressed this idea as follows: "In spite of the industrious spirit which looks for innovation in objects, who does not prefer the circular form to the polygonal for a human face? Who does not believe that the shape of a man's back must provide the type of the back of a chair?"[34] In essence, for de Quincy, type was deeply tied to common patterns of behavior passed down from the past and was an a priori concept embedded in human thought long before "architecture" as we know it existed. Thus, type can be understood as the "first perception" of an object, signifying its common principle.

In summary, late 18th-century Europe experienced rapid political and economic changes driven by the French Revolution and the rise of the bourgeoisie. These shifts fostered a growing need for, and the development of, more modern ways of thinking. Such societal transformations also impacted architecture, leading to the decline of the Vitruvian legacy.

Quatremère de Quincy believed that art and architecture needed to adapt to this new society. In the process, he naturally redefined the origins of art, including the concepts of "imitation" and "beauty." As discussed earlier, his conclusion was that the act of "universalizing" and "generalizing" was closer to the essence of beauty, which he saw as the origin of art and architecture.

This perspective shifted the understanding of beauty from being tied to predetermined proportions or principles of nature to something common and flexible, capable of adapting to the unique conditions of different cultures. For de Quincy, the concept of type encapsulated this adaptability and also served as a tool for categorizing architectural works.

31 de Quincy, "Essay on Imitation," p.308

32 Jacoby, "Reasoning of Architecture," p.80

33 Ibid., p.87

34 de Quincy, "Dictionnaire Historique de l'Architecture" (Paris, 1832), p.630

WALTER GROPIUS: "TYPE IS A STANDARD OF THE AGE"

The 18th and 19th centuries marked a transformative period leading to the emergence of modern society, while the 20th century witnessed its full realization alongside rapid industrialization. This era gave rise to modernism, a movement defined by a critical engagement with past traditions—either accepting or rejecting them—to forge a new aesthetic aligned with industrialization, mass production, and machinery.

In the discourse on modernism in architecture, one cannot overlook the pivotal role of the Bauhaus and its founding director, Walter Gropius. In his influential book *The New Architecture and the Bauhaus*, Gropius advocated for a decisive break from historical traditions, reimagining the architectural concept of type. While de Quincy associated type with history and tradition, Gropius redefined it as "the typical," encapsulating the essence of a specific era. This shift in meaning underscores Gropius's commitment to aligning architectural practice with the evolving needs and values of modern industrial society.[35] Gropius's concept of the typical referred to a "standard" that most effectively embodied the spirit of the times. Consequently, he viewed architecture as a "product" of industrialization, shaped by the technological and cultural shifts of the modern era.[36] In other words, for Gropius, type did not signify a specific formal structure but rather an "image" and a "mode of production" that most efficiently captured the essence of a society.

Contemporary movements, such as digital and parametric architecture, can be viewed as manifestations of the type Gropius described—one that reflects the technologies and ethos of a new era. However, Gropius's concept of type reveals inherent limitations. The effort to propose standards aligned with the spirit of the times often risks devolving into a pursuit of endless novelty. Furthermore, the lack of a consistent one-to-one relationship between specific forms and technologies complicates the task of linking a universally communicable physical entity to a type. Consequently, Gropius's notion of type untethered from formal structures and subject to continual redefinition with each era becomes difficult to uphold as an appropriate concept for common architecture.

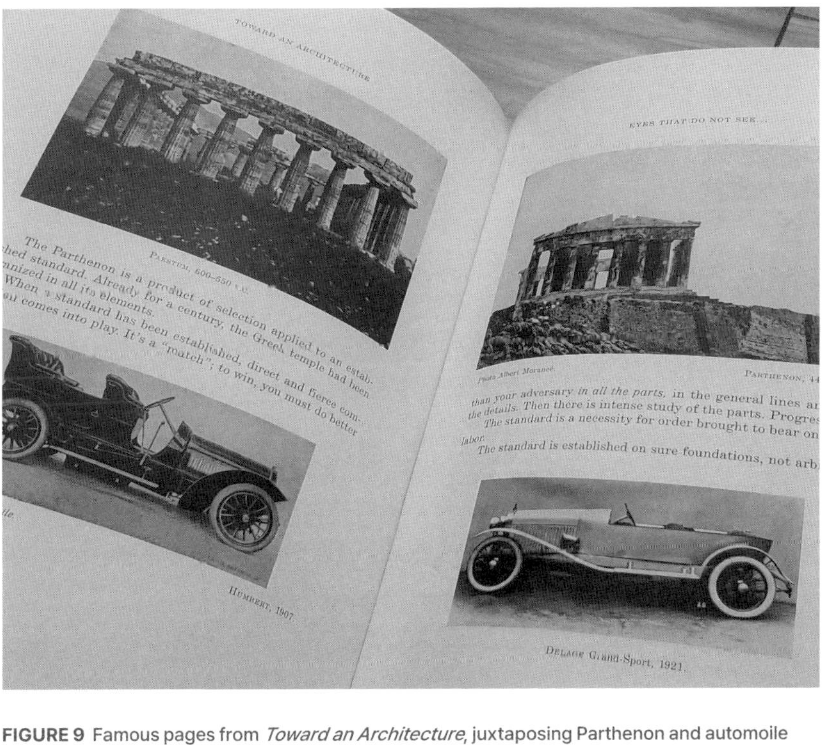

FIGURE 9 Famous pages from *Toward an Architecture*, juxtaposing Parthenon and automoile

FIGURE 10 Prefabricated Copper Houses

35 Jacoby, "The Reasoning of Architecture," p.12

36 Lathouri, "The City as a Project: Types, Typical Objects and Typologies," p.25, *Architectural Design*, No.209, 2011

GIULIO CARLO ARGAN: "TYPE IS A POSTERIORI"

> The notion of the vagueness or generality of the "type"—which cannot therefore directly affect the design of buildings or their formal quality, also explains its generation, the way in which a type is formed. It is never formulated a priori but always deduced from a series of instances.[37]
>
> **GIULIO CARLO ARGAN**

As previously discussed, modernism, championed by figures like Gropius, sought to break from historical tradition. However, after the 1950s, a counter-reaction emerged, characterized by a renewed respect for history and the deliberate integration of historical examples into architectural practice. This shift necessitated a reevaluation of the concept of type, which Gropius had defined as the "standard of a new society." Addressing this need, Giulio Carlo Argan offered a reinterpretation of type in his influential 1963 essay, "On The Typology Of Architecture."

In this essay, Argan critically examines de Quincy's concept of type, posing the question: "For Quatremère de Quincy, type is a priori and can be described as the human perception of an object itself. However, if no definitive forms could be associated with a specific 'type,' how could one define a particular 'type' as such in the first place?" No matter how much a type may be conceived as an a priori concept embodying social and cultural values, it cannot be perceived without an associated physical form. In other words, the very recognition of a type presupposes the existence of a shared formal structure among buildings within a specific cultural context. For Argan, therefore, type is not derived from an a priori but is instead an empirical concept that needs to be "detected" through the comparison and analysis of multiple buildings.

37 G. C. Argan, "On the Typology of Architecture," *Architectural Design*, Dec. 1963, trans. Joseph Rykwart

ALDO ROSSI:
"TYPE IS A UNIT TO READ A CITY"

Typology presents itself as the study of types of elements that cannot be further reduced, elements of a city as well as of an architecture...no type can be identified with only one form, even if all architectural forms are reducible to types. The process of reduction is a necessary, logical operation, and it is impossible to talk about problems of form without this presupposition. In this sense, all architectural theories are also theories of typology.[38]

ALDO ROSSI

The concept of type discussed thus far has functioned either as a tool for analyzing architecture comprehensively or as a fundamental value of architecture itself. For Aldo Rossi, however, the type served as a unit for integratively interpreting both architecture and the city, acting as a conceptual bridge between the two. This perspective resonates with the Alberti's assertion that "the city is like a large house, and the house is like a small city."[39] However, to understand why Rossi was compelled to interpret a complex organism like the city through architecture and type—concepts inherently tied to form—it is essential to consider his historical context.

In the aftermath of the two World Wars, Europe faced the pressing challenge of reconstructing war-torn cities and providing housing for countless displaced populations. This necessity spurred a wave of state-led urban projects that diverged markedly from the traditional fabric of historic European cities. Historically, deeply rooted cities in both the East and West reflected a convergence of "morphological layers" and "historical layers," with their physical forms serving as living records of history and daily life. In contrast, many of the post-war planned cities of the 1950s and 1960s exhibited a clear disconnection between these layers. Addressing this disjunction became a central concern for Aldo Rossi. For Rossi, type represented a formal structure, encapsulating the behaviors, traditions, and history of a culture or region. Due to this accumulated and collective intelligence, type offered a means to reintegrate the fragmented layers of history and form across architecture and city scales.

In summary, for Rossi, type extended beyond the individual intentions of the architect, serving as a conceptual framework for addressing comprehensive and fundamental questions about the creative processes underlying architecture and city.[40] To analyze cities and architecture "comprehensively," Rossi argued for the necessity of addressing buildings in both formal and individual terms. The analytical framework that enabled this dual perspective was type. The most compelling aspect of Rossi's concept of type lies in its capacity to mediate the tension between "generality" and "individuality," representing a significant evolution from the earlier interpretations by de Quincy and Argan.

38 Rossi, "The Architecture of the City," p.41

39 Alberti, "On the Art of Building in Ten Books," p.23

40 Refer to Pier Vittorio Aureli's AA School Lecture: Theory and Ethos: Towards a Common Architectural Language Part 6 (2012)

RAFAEL MONEO: "TYPE IS REPETITIVE"

On the one hand, a work of architecture has to be considered in its own right, as an entity in itself. That is, like other forms of art, it can be characterized by a condition of uniqueness...On the other hand, a work of architecture can also be seen as belonging to a class of repeated objects, characterized, like a class of tools or instruments, by some general attributes.[41]

RAFAEL MONEO

The concept of type in architecture, as discussed thus far, has primarily functioned as a tool for analyzing buildings or as a logical framework for defining the discipline of architecture, rather than as a practical design instrument. However, Rafael Moneo reinterprets type as a practical tool for design. He asserts that type serves as a rational and common starting point for architectural creation, providing a foundation for systematic exploration and innovation.[42] Why, then, does Moneo argue that type should serve as the starting point for design? As reflected in his initial assertion, he perceives architecture as more akin to a functional tool than a work of art. Functional objects integrate deeply into daily life, and their formal structures recur over time. For example, while individual hammer designs may vary, their basic function remains constant, resulting in a shared formal structure. Similarly, despite frequent criticisms, the form of East Asian apartments endures due to their economic and political utility. For Moneo, this recurring formal structure embodies the essence of type, which he views as both rational and practical, making it a logical and effective foundation for architectural creation.

Moneo's concept of type as related to repetition appears to have been significantly influenced by the George Kubler and his seminal work, *The Shape Of Time*. In the chapter titled "Linked Solutions," Kubler posits that tools can be understood as solutions to specific problems. Rather than being entirely replaced as society and technology evolve, these solutions often serve as foundations for subsequent iterations. Their core formal structures persist through a sequential progression, enabling continuity and adaptation over time.[43] Architecture, as a vessel for human life, inherently incorporates formal structures that are both repetitive and continuous. These qualities of "repeatability" and "continuity" align seamlessly with Moneo's interpretation of type.[44]

In essence, the value of type lies in its resistance to rapid change in the face of societal or technological shifts; instead, it evolves gradually, mirroring the pace of life. For Moneo, type embodies the enduring value of solutions that persist beneath the transformations of form over time. This durability makes type not only the most rational and reliable starting point for common architecture but also a flexible framework, capable of adapting to the evolving needs of each era.

41 Moneo, "On Typology," p.23

42 Ibid., p.37

43 Kubler, "The Shape of Time," p.28-55

44 Refer to Rafael Moneo's 2014 AA School Lecture, Type vs. Typology - Keynote speech

TYPE AND FUNCTIONALISM

So far, we have briefly explored how the concept of type has evolved within architectural history, focusing on definitions proposed by various architects. Despite its shifting interpretations, one constant characteristic of type is its lack of direct association with function. At first glance, the notion that function is unrelated to type—a core framework for classifying architecture—may appear counterintuitive. However, asserting that type is independent of function does not diminish the importance of functionality in architecture. Instead, it underscores the logical flaws in elevating function as the central criterion for architectural classification or value systems.

Rafael Moneo critiques the limitations of functionalism in architecture, stating: "If architecture is about solving specific requirements and expressing them in form, then architecture becomes a discipline that seeks the right answers to specific problems. This would mean that the correct answer always results in the same form. However, the architectural design process is never this linear." As such, functionalism waned in architectural discourse, with even its proponents often prioritizing the symbolic representation of "functionalism" over the creation of forms dictated purely by function.

Function is undoubtedly one of the key values in architecture. However, as demonstrated by the varied forms a hotel can take—such as a courtyard layout, a single-loaded corridor design, or a tower configuration—a single function can result in multiple architectural forms. This variability highlights the inherent limitations of analyzing architecture solely through the lens of function. Ironically, such a narrow approach lacks versatility and proves inadequate for fostering common communication within the field.

While architecture must address technical conditions and problem-solving requirements, it is also a medium for expressing the architect's values and perspectives on society in an "architectural" manner. Consequently, the ability to effectively communicate these values and their commonness becomes a critical aspect of architectural discourse.

FIGURE 11 Lloyd's Building represnts functionalism symbolically

5
VALUES OF TYPE

TYPE: LINK BETWEEN CREATIVITY AND HISTORY

If...forms by themselves are relatively empty of meaning, it follows that the forms which we intuit will, in the unconscious mind, tend to attract to themselves certain associations of meaning. This could not only mean that we are not free from the forms of the past, and from the availability of these forms as typological models, but that, if we assume we are free, we have lost control over a very active sector of our imagination, and of our power to communicate with others.[45]

ALAN COLQUHOUN

The values of type discussed in this book can be broadly categorized into three key aspects: historicity, abstraction, and repetition. This chapter focuses on the first of these—historicity. For a formal structure to be recognized and communicated as a type, it must endure over an extended period and gain acceptance by a majority of society as common. Thus, the value of type lies not in its instrumentality or practical utility but in the messages and familiarity conveyed through its historical record. This perspective underscores that architecture's value extends beyond the brilliance of individual architects, encompassing its broader significance and connection to collective cultural memory.

Type, as the culmination of historical layers embodied in physical form, transcends being a superficial shell that merely showcases traditional imagery. Instead, as the initial quote suggests, it is a structural form that encapsulates and preserves meanings attributed to it over time. Moreover, solutions to new challenges often draw from types that addressed similar issues in the past. In this sense, type acts as a bridge, linking the past to the moment of creation and extending that connection to the future.

In essence, the value of type lies in its continuity, which unites the past, present, and future. However, this continuity does not imply an uncritical reverence for history and tradition. If type were merely retrospective, it would be confined to reflecting on the past without engaging with the present or future. Instead, in a rapidly changing society, type exists in a dynamic tension between the forces of tradition, which resist change, and those of radicalism, which demand it. Within this context, history serves as a collective repository of solutions, offering a balanced framework for value judgments and common responses to emerging challenges.

Furthermore, type's ability to connect historical precedents with moments of creation provides a rational lens through which to approach and analyze forthcoming changes. By bridging temporal boundaries, type equips architects to engage with the future in a thoughtful and informed manner.

Since the receiver of a signal becomes its sender in the normal course of historical transmission (e.g., the discoverer of a document usually is its editor), we may treat receivers and senders together under the heading of relays. Each relay is the occasion of some deformation in the original signal. Certain details seem insignificant and they are dropped in the relay; others have an importance conferred by their relationship to events occurring in the moment of the relay, and so they are exaggerated.[46]

GEORGE KUBLER

45 Colquhoun, "Typology and Design Method," p.74, *Perspecta* 12 (1969)
46 Kubler, "The Shape of Time," 1962, p.19

PAST IS ALWAYS AROUND US

Le passé ne sert qu'à connaître l'actualité. Mais l'actualité m'échappe. Qu'est-ce que c'est donc que l'actualité?
HENRI FOCILLON

The reality we perceive is, in essence, a composition of messages from the past. What we know and see does not come from "now" but "then," not "here" but "there."[47] These messages, originating from another time and place, surround us constantly, each carrying its own story and speaking to us in its unique way. Inspiration, therefore, is rarely a purely internal process. Rather, it is a fortuitous moment when the most relevant message among those surrounding us reveals itself. In the history of art, sudden shifts often occur when an unexpected message from the distant past emerges as particularly resonant.

These messages from the past do not present themselves in an orderly sequence, waiting for entry into our consciousness. Instead, multiple pasts coexist around us, perpetually intersecting. In architecture, types serve as these enduring messages from history. Consequently, if we were to distill our environment to its essence, it would not be inaccurate to describe our world and its history as a tapestry composed of types.

Among the multitude of messages that types convey, the architect's act of selecting and reinterpreting one to suit the present becomes a means of crafting a message for the future. Thus, the value of type is most profoundly realized at the moment it serves as a bridge, connecting the past to the future.

47 Kubler, "The Shape of Time," 1962, p.15

WHY ABSTRACTION?

It is through abstraction, understood as the process through which man seeks to define generic frameworks rather than specific solutions.[48]

ALEJANDRA CELEDON

The second core value of type is its abstraction. The term "abstract" derives from the Latin word *trahere*, meaning "to pull something essential out of the totality of which it is a part."[49] This etymology highlights that abstraction is not confined to a specific style, such as "abstract painting" in art. Rather, it reflects a fundamental instinct of human intelligence to identify commonalities and essence within the diverse and complex phenomena of reality.[50]

Abstract thinking, therefore, is an essential tool for navigating and understanding our complex world. The abstraction inherent in types holds a pivotal role in architecture, enabling the discipline to distill varied information and design ideas into commonly comprehensible formal structures. This capacity for abstraction makes architecture socially accessible and intelligible, establishing it as a defining and indispensable characteristic of type.

It is through the diagrammatic, and therefore generalizing, abstraction of type that an artist is able to speculate beyond the limitations of the physical world.[51]

SAM JACOBY

The abstract approach in architecture has been a cornerstone of the discipline for centuries. In *Lineaments*, the first book of Alberti's ten-volume treatise *De Re Aedificatoria*, he asserts that abstraction holds greater importance than physical construction or materials in architecture. Alberti's concept of *lineaments* refers to principles that, while invisible, form the organizational framework of a building. These principles possess commonness, enabling their application across multiple architectural works.[52]

In his view, *lineaments* require architects to move beyond the physical limitations of materials and construction to uncover the deeper logic of design. For Alberti, *lineaments* liberated architects from the constraints of physical conditions and materials, functioning simultaneously as a demonstration of design logic and as the logic itself.

In modern times, Le Corbusier similarly highlighted the importance of "regulating lines" as a key concept in creating order within architectural design. Regulating lines share similarities with Alberti's *lineaments* in that both emphasize the underlying logic, rules, and structural principles that govern the design process rather than the resulting form.

Abstraction, therefore, has a long history in architecture, consistently playing a critical role in establishing and revealing the principles and logic of design. For communication grounded in coherent logic, abstraction is indispensable. Through abstraction, architects can convey the underlying reasoning that guides their designs, fostering understanding and dialogue.

This underscores why abstraction is essential in architecture and why its result—type—is a foundational concept for common architecture. Type embodies the abstraction of diverse architectural phenomena into universally intelligible structures, making it a vital tool for creating common ground for communication in architecture.

48 Celedon, "The Plan as Eidos," p.4

49 http://languages.oup.com/google-dictionary-en/

50 Refer to Pier Vittorio Aureli's 2013 Lecture AA School: Design without Qualities Part 1

51 Jacoby, "The Reasoning of Architecture," p.101

52 Alberti, "On the Art of the Building in Ten Books," p.7

ABSTRACTION: POTENTIAL NEWNESS

Thus one should not say (or at least one would be wrong to say) that a statute, or the composition of a finished and rendered picture, has served as the type for the copy that one made. But when a fragment, a sketch, the thought of a master, a more or less vague description has given the birth to a work of art in the imagination of an artist, one will say that the type has been furnished for him by such an idea, motif, or intention.[53]

QUATREMERE DE QUINCY

A type represents the essential formal structure of architecture, revealed only when elements of a completed building—such as materials, ambiance, and ornamentation—are stripped away. This process of abstraction endows type with the potential to evolve into diverse designs. In other words, its abstract nature renders type both a common and practical tool for communication, while simultaneously providing space for subjective interpretation by the architect, fostering innovation. As such, type emerges as a complex concept, balancing commonness and creativity.

An intriguing dimension of type's abstraction becomes apparent when it is expressed through language rather than form. For instance, the word "chair" evokes the essential idea of a chair, rather than a specific design such as the Thonet Chair. However, when type is represented visually, the universality of its structural concept risks being overshadowed, as perception may become limited to a single, concrete image. If type is reduced to a specific form or image, it ceases to function as an abstract framework, thereby diminishing opportunities for subjective engagement and interpretation.

Its abstraction, most effectively conveyed through language, naturally aligns type with common communication. Paradoxically, while type is an architectural concept, its essence is often better articulated in linguistic terms.

By doing so, type preserves its commoness and flexibility, maintaining its core essence while fostering understanding and dialogue across diverse contexts.

This purging of formal specificity and the associated value judgment of models before they become formally "vague" types, de-historicizes form and makes it possible to creatively determine a new value.[54]

SAM JACOBY

53 de Quincy, "Encyclopedie Methodique," *Architecture*, vol.3, pt. 2 (1825)
54 Jacoby, "The Reasoning of Architecture," p.220

FORM AND FORMAL STRUCTURE

In discussing the abstraction of type, I have deliberately used the term "formal structure" rather than simply "form." While "form" is easily associated with perceptual recognition—what is seen—"formal structure" pertains to conceptual understanding—what is known. In *The Formal Basis Of Modern Architecture*, Peter Eisenman categorizes formal structures into centroidal and linear types. Although this represents a more extreme abstraction than type, the concept shares a fundamental similarity: both seek to identify the core formal structures shared across multiple buildings.

To appreciate why the results of abstraction—formal structures—differ from forms, and why formal structure holds value, we must examine how humans perceive and interpret their environment. When we observe our surroundings, we initially experience them as undifferentiated information. Human intellect plays a crucial role in comparing, analyzing, and organizing this information into shared structures that facilitate common communication. A clear example of this intellectual process is found in school subjects like mathematics, geography, or physics, which classify vast phenomena into systems that promote common understanding and exchange.

In architecture, formal structures operate as such a system, enabling common communication. While individual architectural elements—such as materials, window shapes, or ornamental details—may differ significantly, the formal structure represents the shared essence distilled from analyzing the forms of various buildings. This essence can be likened to the "DNA" of architecture, and it underscores the distinction between form and formal structure. Form, in this context, derives its value from individuality and the unique characteristics of a specific building or design. Conversely, formal structure holds value in its universality and inclusivity, abstracting and generalizing the common traits of diverse architectural forms.

Formal structures are thus indispensable for fostering shared understanding and dialogue within architecture. They encapsulate the core principles and organizational patterns that unify diverse designs, providing a foundation for a common architectural language.

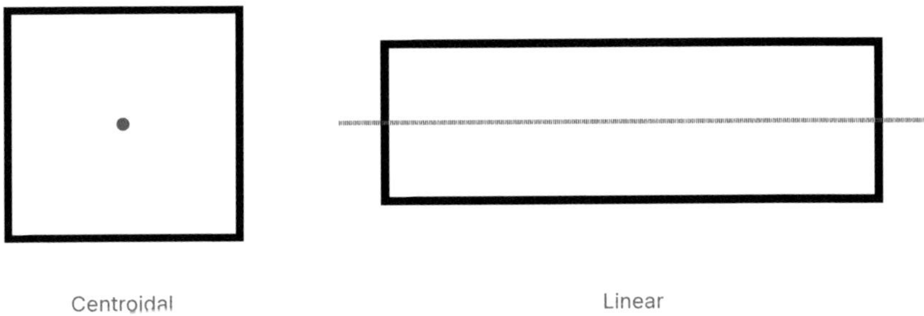

FIGURE 12

REPETITION IS NOT REPLICATION

Type is a medium of non-imitative reproduction.[55]

SAM JACOBY

Now, we turn to the third and final value of type: repetition. Significant architectural works serve not only as indicators of the cultural and societal conditions of their time but also as the outcomes of prolonged contemplation and problem-solving efforts. For any given problem, multiple solutions often emerge. For example, in postwar Korea, the housing crisis was addressed through a variety of building types, including mixed-use residential building and duplex buildings, row houses, and apartment complexes. Among these, apartment complex type proved to be the most effective solution and were repeatedly implemented, eventually solidifying their status as a unique type of Korea.

As societal transformations shift the problems that architecture seeks to address, types are continually revitalized through the innovative solutions being developed. Architect Hwang Doo-jin's Rainbow Rice Cake Architecture exemplifies how systematic innovation can be achieved through the repetition inherent in types. Hwang Doo-jin, in addressing Korea's urban and housing challenges of today, conducted a meticulous analysis of the mixed-use residential building type around 1950~1970s, which was rendered obsolete by the apartment type, reinterpreting it for contemporary contexts through his concept of Rainbow Rice Cake Architecture. Building upon the familiar type of post Korean War era, Hwang's approach preserves their recognizability while introducing adaptations suited to contemporary needs. The result is a formal structure that embodies both commonness and innovation.

This formal structure is not merely a design outcome but a reflection of the logic of composition tailored to Korean society. Its inclusivity and universality enable it to be repeatedly applied across diverse building projects. In this sense, type is intrinsically linked to repetition, with repetition serving as the mechanism through which type achieves commonness.

Furthermore, type allows architecture to transcend the constraints of authorship that have historically shaped its narrative. Architectural history is often portrayed as a succession of works by celebrated architects, emphasizing the "uniqueness" and "individuality" of their designs. Type, however, moves beyond such personal distinctions, functioning as an intellectual framework that facilitates a common understanding of urban and architectural history. By shifting focus from individual creativity to shared structural principles, type offers a lens through which to view architecture as a collective and enduring endeavor.

Rossi uses repetition as a strategy of rationalization, in which typological recurrence is a mechanism to strip away meaning until architecture becomes "silent," which points to a desire to both regain and ahistoricize the past as a new event.[56]

MARY LOUISE LOBSINGER

55 Jacoby, "The Reasoning of Architecture," p.8

56 Lobsinger, "That Obscure Object of Desire," p.38-61

6
TYPOLOGICAL APPROACH

TYPE AND TYPOLOGICAL APPROACH

[T]ypologies allow one to make use of knowledge about past solutions to related architectural problems.[57]

PETER ROWE

A type represents patterns or absolute standards,[58] while a typological approach refers to the effort to uncover the unchanging principles behind objects and phenomena. Although these concepts may appear similar, they are fundamentally different, and the distinction between "type" and "typological approach" is particularly significant in East Asian cultures, where the history of architecture as a scholarly discipline is relatively brief.

In Western culture, architecture has been regarded as an academic discipline since Roman times, with written texts documenting its principles and practices. This historical context created an intellectual environment conducive to recording, analyzing, and studying various architectural types. In contrast, East Asia traditionally viewed architecture as inseparable from "building" or "construction." This perspective reflects a limited familiarity with thinking about architecture in typological or abstract terms and underscores the absence of a framework for developing diverse types. While these differences are rooted in historical and cultural contexts, the value of the typological approach remains universally applicable, including in East Asia.

To illustrate the typological approach, consider the example of shoes. Over time, shoes have been classified into increasingly specialized categories—dress shoes, boots, golf shoes, basketball shoes—each evolving in design and functionality. Yet the type "shoe" retains an unchanging core value, providing a common image that facilitates communication. The typological approach, therefore, does not focus on the visual image or design of individual shoes but rather seeks to explore the original intent and intellectual framework behind their creation—what might be called their core essence.

In architecture, this entails analyzing the overarching formal structure of a building and its historical context, rather than assuming that typological development occurs merely through alterations in details such as window shapes, roof profiles, or exterior materials. This inherent complexity makes employing a typological approach as a design methodology a demanding task. However, the intellectual environment fostered by the typological approach transcends time and authorship, democratizing the design process and making it accessible to a broader audience. In this way, the typological approach serves as a method for sharing architectural knowledge, positioning it as a powerful tool for creating universally accessible and common architecture.

Architectural typology is comparable to iconography as a reinvention of past images, themes, and values within a contemporary context.[59]

SAM JACOBY

57 Rowe, "A Priori Knowledge and Heuristics Reasoning in Architectural Design," JAE, 36.1, p.19, 1982
58 Jacoby, "The Reasoning of Architecture," p.92
59 Ibid., p.220

GENERAL FORM VS. SPECIFIC FORM

One imitates nature by making as she makes, that is, not by repeating her work properly speaking, but by appropriating the principles that served as a rule for this work, in other words, her spirit, her intentions and her laws.[60]

QUATREMERE DE QUINCY

Previously, we examined the general value of the typological approach. In this section, let's focus specifically on its value as a design methodology. Every resultant form begins with a simple and general form, which may represent a type or take the shape of pure geometry. This general form serves as a reference point during its development into a specific form, and the transformation must occur without compromising the essential characteristics of the original.[61] For instance, if functional requirements necessitate alterations that disrupt the fundamental structure of the general form—such as a single-loaded corridor type—it may be more effective to begin anew with a different general form, such as a courtyard type, centralized type, or tower type.

When analyzing a building, the first step in the design process is to strip away specific details to identify its general form. This approach allows for tracing the design logic that led to the final outcome and ensures that the foundational conditions for commonness are established.

Le Corbusier's "Five Points of Architecture" and "Four Compositions" exemplify the typological approach as a design methodology. He captured the spirit of modernity—defined by industrialization and new materials—through the general form of the Maison Dom-ino (Figure 13). His "Five Points" (Figure 14) and "Four Compositions" (Figure 15) offered specific interpretations that expanded and refined this general form. Critiquing the Western classical architecture, which relied on walls as structural elements, Le Corbusier introduced the post-lintel system of the Maison Dom-ino as a

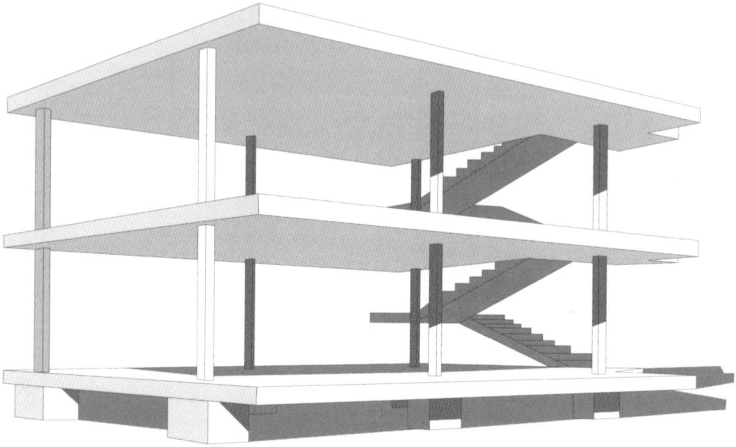

FIGURE 13 Maison Dom-Ino

general form to liberate walls from structural functions. This separation provided far greater flexibility in modern architecture compared to traditional practices, where partition walls were inextricably tied to structural demands.

Among Le Corbusier's Five Points, the most significant—the free plan—emerges directly from the general form of the Maison Dom-ino and provides a conceptual foundation for developing specific forms. His "Four Compositions" further illustrate methods to implement the logic of the free plan. Notably, Composition #3 from Figure 15 develops the general form of Dom-ino, demonstrating the freedom of wall placement to create specific forms that embody its inherent logic.

Le Corbusier's work underscores the importance of respecting the original general form when transforming it into specific forms that exist in reality. Neglecting this foundational step risks undermining the logical coherence of the design. Such a lapse erodes the critical values of type—commonness and communicative capacity—which are essential for fostering shared understanding in architecture.

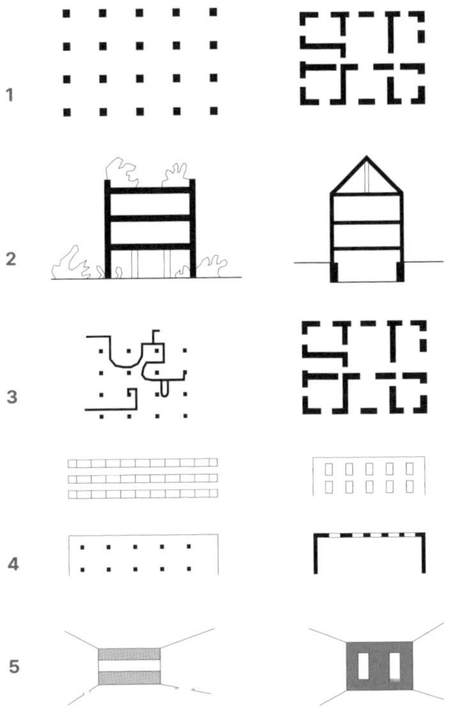

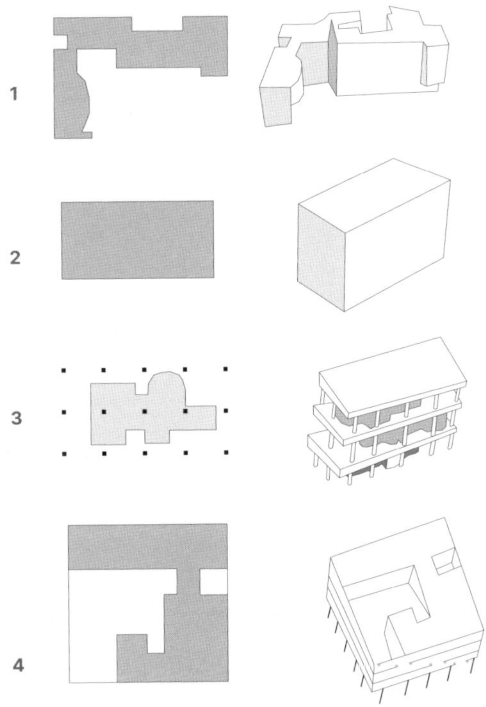

FIGURE 14 (LEFT) Le Corbusier's Five Points emphasize the principles of independent structure and the free plan, encapsulated well in point 1 and 3. These principles serve as specific forms

FIGURE 15 (RIGHT) Le Corbusier's Four Compositions

60 de Quincy, "Essay on Imitation," p.230
61 Eisenman, "The Formal Basis of Modern Architecture," p.85-87

7 EXAMPLES OF TYPOLOGICAL APPROACH

The typological approach discussed earlier prioritizes the starting point and developmental process of a design over its final result. As a consequence, even if resultant forms appear identical, they cannot be classified as the same type if their underlying motivations and structural logic differ. The "grid" is a prime example of a type that, while visually similar, can emerge from distinct motivations and structural principles. The most common interpretation of the grid is as a network of pathways designed to optimize the distribution of resources. Additionally, its uniform, non-hierarchical structure is often associated with notions of political egalitarianism. Archaeological evidence suggests that grid-based urban and structural systems have been in use since the advent of settled societies. These systems likely originated as tools for efficiently dividing land.[62] From this, we can identify two primary motivations behind the creation of grids: 1. To provide a form that ensures universal agreement on land ownership, and 2. To offer a universal template that facilitates coexistence and collaboration.[63]

In ancient Greece, the grid was employed as a tool for what we might now describe as new town development. During this period, state expansion often occurred through warfare, an economically costly endeavor. To incentivize participation, the state distributed conquered lands among its citizens, and the grid provided an efficient template for equitable land division. This distribution was guided by the principle of *isonomia*, meaning equality before the law, symbolizing fairness in resource allocation. As such, the political and economic significance of the grid in ancient Greece was not vastly different from how it is understood today.[64]

However, Hippodamus, a Greek philosopher and urban planner, introduced a significant departure from this egalitarian ideal. He divided citizens into three distinct classes—artists, farmers, and soldiers—and categorized land into three corresponding types: sacred spaces, everyday spaces, and private spaces. In this arrangement, everyday spaces were allocated to farmers, who bore the responsibility of providing sustenance for the other classes.[65] This system reveals a clear deviation from the principle of isonomia, as it introduced a hierarchical structure that undermined equality.

Hippodamus preserved the physical structure of the grid but infused it with a class-based functionality. This transformed the grid from a symbol of *isonomia* into a mechanism of hierarchical stratification. While the structural form of the grid remained consistent, its intent and underlying logic shifted dramatically.

This contrast demonstrates that even when formal structures appear identical, the differing motivations and generative logics behind them can create fundamentally distinct types. The isonomia-based grid and the Hippodamian grid serve as compelling examples of how the same physical framework can embody opposing social and political values.

The duality of the grid persisted across eras, adapting to reflect the values and motivations of each period. During the Roman Empire, the grid structure incorporated a hierarchical dimension through the *cardo* and *decumanus*, two principal axes that intersected to form a cross-like structure at the center of Roman cities. These axes symbolized Rome's logic of colonial expansion, functioning as highways that facilitated rapid territorial growth. Their prominence reflected Rome's military strategy and the political transition from the Republic to the Empire.[66] The hierarchical nature of the cardo and decumanus contrasted with the more egalitarian Greek-style grid used for planning the areas surrounding these central axes. This created a hybrid urban structure: a macro-grid defined by the cardo and decumanus for imperial and military purposes, and a micro-grid designed to serve the everyday needs of the general populace.

In the American colonial era, the grid was employed as a tool of expropriation, influenced by concepts like the enclosure movement, popularized by thinkers such as John Locke. According to enclosure philosophy, land was deemed valuable only when cultivated, and cultivation was viewed both

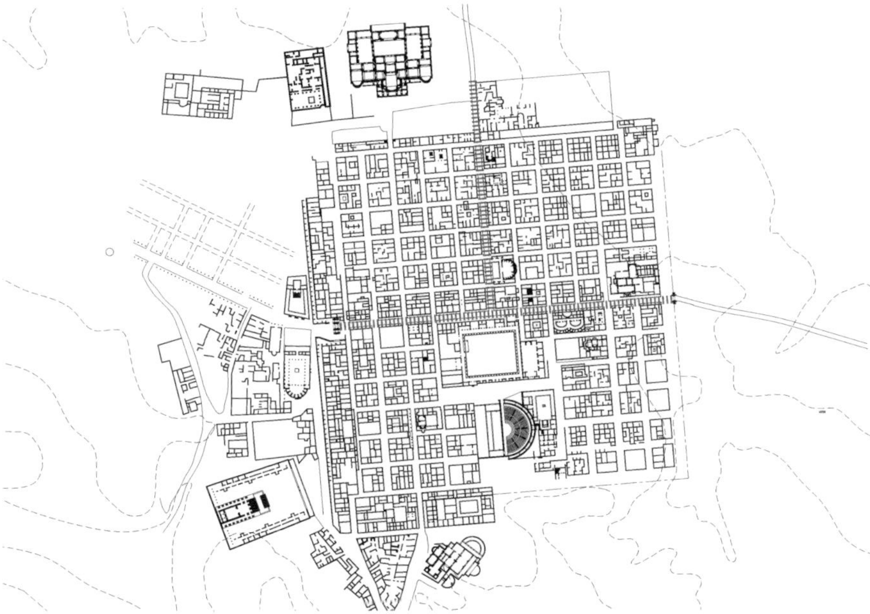

FIGURE 16 Timgad, the urban structure of the Cardo and Decumanus

as a moral duty and a justification for ownership. The British perceived the North American continent as "empty" land and claimed it by subdividing it into grids, which were then allocated to settlers. This logic echoed practices from ancient Greece and Rome, where states delegated the responsibilities of land cultivation and ownership to individuals.[67]

Thus, while the grid consistently served as a framework for organizing land, its purposes and implications varied significantly. In ancient Rome, the grid symbolized imperial dominance and military efficiency. In the American colonies, it became a mechanism for territorial conquest and dispossession. These variations demonstrate the enduring adaptability of the grid as a typological framework, shaped by the values and motivations of the societies that employed it.

Contrary to the common architectural assumption that the grid has been employed for millennia due to its "rationality" and "egalitarianism," it has often served as a tool and formal template for the violent act of colonial land subdivision. Even in modern cities, these divisions persist in cadastral maps, where boundaries function as legal demarcations that frequently incite competition and conflict.[68]

Recognizing this historical context underscores that the grid cannot be reduced to a singular type to be applied indiscriminately. A typological approach requires a thoughtful process that incorporates the historical and cultural knowledge surrounding a given structural form. By engaging in this process, architects can deploy types with greater precision and creativity, while also effectively communicating their deeper meaning and implications to others.

62 Aureli, "Appropriation, Subdivison," *Abstraction: A Political History of the Urban Grid*, 2018

63 Nigel Goring-Morris and Belfer-Cohen, "A Roof over One's Head: Developments in Near Eastern Residential Architecture across the Epipaleolithic Neolithic Transition"

64 Vernant, "Myth and Thought among the Greeks," Janet Lloyd and Jeff Fort, 2006

65 Mazza, "Plan and Constitution - Aristotle's Hippodamus: Towards an Ostensive Definition of Spatial Planning," *The Town Planning Review* 80, no.2, 2009, p.113-141

66 Morley, "Cities in Context: Urban Systems in Roman Italy, Roman Urbanism: Beyond the Consumer City edited by Parkins (Routledge: London, 2005)," p. 42-58

67 Aureli, "Appropriation, Subdivision, Abstraction: A Political History of the Urban Grid," 2018, p.142-148

68 Ibid., p.155-160

HOUSING

Much like the grid, the apartment type has evolved through two contrasting historical models. In Korea, apartments emerged in the post Korean War period as a solution to the urgent need for efficient housing supply. Confronted with financial constraints, the government delegated large-scale land development to private entities. These private developers, driven primarily by the pursuit of maximum profit, established the "complex-style" apartment culture that continues to define modern Korean housing until today.[69] In contrast, Soviet apartments were developed under the ideological banner of constructing a "communist way of life," aiming to provide housing that allowed all citizens to live equally. Despite originating from an entirely opposing economic system—communism—the resultant Soviet communal housing closely paralleled the Korean model, giving rise to the "microdistrict" apartment type.

Both Korea and the Soviet Union faced similar challenges following major conflicts—World War I and the Korean War, respectively—with the urgent task of providing housing for rapidly growing urban populations. In the Soviet Union, apartments were not the immediate solution. Following the February Revolution, the central government confiscated aristocratic and bourgeois mansions, redistributing them for use by multiple families. Each family was assigned a single room, while kitchens and bathrooms were shared as communal facilities. This arrangement caused significant inconvenience and compromised basic privacy.

To address these inadequate living conditions and standardize housing for workers, the Soviet Union, under Nikita Khrushchyov's leadership in the 1950s, initiated large-scale production of complex-style apartments. Similarly, Korea experimented with various housing types, including mixed-use residential buildings (*sangga-jutaek*) and Western style single-family and duplex houses, locally known as *yangok*. After these early trials, large-scale

FIGURE 17 Apartment Complex of Seoul in 1976

complex-style apartment developments began in earnest during the 1970s, eventually becoming the dominant residential type in Korea.[70]

In both contexts, efforts to improve substandard living conditions led to the widespread adoption of the "complex-style apartment" as the most practical solution. This type emerged as a natural response to the pressing housing demands of the time, shaped by the socio-economic conditions in each country.

The purposes and intended outcomes of apartment construction differed significantly between the Soviet Union and Korea. When the Soviet Union launched its large-scale apartment projects, Nikita Khrushchyov heralded the complex-style apartment as an ideal model for realizing a communist way of life. He envisioned that shared communal facilities, such as playgrounds, nurseries, and laundries, collectively managed by residents, would foster stronger social bonds and a sense of solidarity.[71] Khrushchyov further anticipated that residents would organize neighborhood watch systems, promoting active collaboration between the people and the government.

In contrast, the development of apartments in Korea was shaped by policies aimed at minimizing government investment in urban infrastructure

FIGURE 18 Microdistricts (Микрорайон, Mikrorayon) in the former Soviet Union

while addressing housing shortages efficiently. This led to the emergence of complex-style apartment developments.[72] Over time, however, these apartments evolved from a pragmatic housing solution into Korea's most secure investment asset and a highly commodified form of real estate. In summary, Soviet apartment complexes served as political tools designed to cultivate a sense of community and promote communist living ideals, whereas Korean apartment complexes prioritized economic efficiency and became prized commodities.

This comparison underscores the importance of understanding the history of the apartment type through a typological approach. Types cannot be defined solely by their physical forms; without considering their cultural and historical contexts, their meanings remain ambiguous. By interpreting the cultural environment, we can uncover the deeper significance and intent behind a given architectural form.

69 박철수, "아파트," 2013
70 Ibid.
71 Harris, "Soviet Mass Housing and the Communist Way of Life," p.181
72 박인석, "아파트 한국 사회," p.8

8
COMPLEMENTARITY BETWEEN TYPES AND EXAMPLES

The effect of type on architecture is displaced and enacted by the model.[73]

SAM JACOBY

As discussed in Chapter 4, type in architecture possesses two opposing characteristics. Quatremère de Quincy argued that type is an absolute and a priori concept, while Giulio Carlo Argan stated that it is something derived a posteriori through analysis. Plato's notion of *geometra* offers a new perspective on this historical debate. Plato described two methods of human knowledge production, with the first being "*geometra*," a discipline based on hypotheses and assumptions. Mathematics is a prime example of this approach, as it assumes operations like addition and subtraction as absolutes and builds all subsequent knowledge upon them.

Type can also be seen as a form of *geometra*. It is a product of assumption rather than an absolute form, and once a type becomes familiar, we instinctively recall an abstract formal structure when we think of it, even if not in concrete detail. Thus, type may lack value as a "specific and tangible form," but its abstract nature allows it to embody a process that is always open to development and concretization. However, as seen in the discussion of "general form vs. specific form," if individual and specific issues are addressed in a fragmented manner without considering the underlying structure of the type, the continuity of the process is lost. This disconnect prevents the type from evolving into a proper specific form and makes the design process unintelligible. A design process that cannot be read is ultimately a failure in communication and thus lacks commonness.

In contrast, examples, due to their specificity and clarity, exist only in the "moment" when they are determined. They do not encompass the process of transformation or development. The act of deciding on an example in design provides relief from the challenges posed by type's continuity.

The etymology of "decision" (*caedere*) means "to cut," implying a severance from the ongoing flow of continuity that existed up to the moment of decision, redirecting focus to the clear form or image presented by the example. This isolatedness of examples is highly instrumental in terms of design. While type's inclusivity and abstraction demand continuity and consistent logic in the design process, which can become constraining, the instrumentality and immediate communicability of examples allow architects to address practical challenges in the design process effectively by relying on existing precedents.

There is often resistance to using existing examples or precedents directly in design, likely due to the difficulty of capturing market attention in a world that constantly demands newness. However, existing examples offer direct or indirect solutions to current or anticipated problems and serve as historical records, providing a value that is more common than mere "newness."

In conclusion, the abstraction of type and the clarity of examples, as well as the continuity of type and the instrumentality of examples, form a complementary pair. Together, they address each other's shortcomings and serve as a practical combination for common architecture. In the next chapter, we will explore the value of examples in architecture in greater detail.

> While a structural concept of architecture relies on persistent types, these are communicated through models.[74]
>
> **SAM JACOBY**

73 Jacoby, "The Reasoning of Architecture," p.235

74 Ibid., p.236

9
CHARACTERISTICS OF EXAMPLE APPROACH

CHARACTERISTIC 1 : FROM THE PARTICULAR TO THE PARTICULAR

In the previous chapter, we briefly outlined the characteristics of examples as a means to complement the limitations of type. For convenience, let us refer to this method of utilizing examples as the "example approach." Aristotle, in his *Prior Analytics*, defined induction as deriving general principles from particular facts and deduction as finding particular facts based on general principles. However, the example approach moves from particular to particular, making it a third form of reasoning that does not belong to either induction or deduction.[75] Therefore, dichotomies such as "part-to-whole" or "generality-specificity" do not exist within the exemplary approach. Instead, it exists solely to express its intended meaning with precision.[76]Architecture, as a discipline, can be described as the act of negotiating tensions between countless dichotomous concepts—such as "concept-reality" and "inside-outside." Within this context, the example approach, as a logic beyond dichotomy, offers a fascinating methodology for design. This is because most designers, including architects, typically begin by establishing an overarching framework and then gradually refine their designs by adding details to this abstract structure. Examples, however, do not require such an intermediate process of concretizing abstract ideas.

The clarity of examples bypasses the abstract-to-concrete translation process and provides a distinct value to the discipline of architecture, one that differs fundamentally from the abstraction of type. By leveraging their inherent specificity and precision, examples contribute to architectural design as a tool for immediate and effective problem-solving, enriching the discourse in ways that type alone cannot achieve.

75 Aristotle, "Prior Analytics," 69a13-15

76 Agamben, "The Signature of All Things," p.19

CHARACTERISTIC 2: INCLUSION BY EXCLUSION

To be capable of acting as an example, the syntagma must be suspended from its normal function.[77]

GIORGIO AGAMBEN

Examples are always exceptional, existing independently rather than being confined to a specific logic.[78] This is the second key characteristic of examples explored in this chapter. What does this mean? At first glance, it may seem that examples are chosen because they share commonalities with the phenomena or principles they aim to illustrate. However, if a particular commonality defined an example, then it would always be recognized as such before being selected.

Instead, examples are formed through clear relationships between a specific situation and an object. For instance, the sound "Shh" used to indicate quietness is only meaningful in the context of a particular social convention; outside of that context, it's just a sound without inherent meaning. Shh is included to function as such by being excluded from its original context: sound. In summary, examples are not defined by inherent commonalities but are instead created through the relationships observed in specific contexts. Depending on these relationships, examples take on exceptional roles that diverge from their original purposes.

This perspective aligns with Robert Venturi's insights in his seminal work, *Complexity and Contradiction in Architecture*, which will be examined in greater detail in Chapter 10. Venturi viewed architectural history as an encyclopedia of examples that could be repurposed as design materials. He extracted examples from their original historical contexts and reinterpreted them to communicate intentional meanings relevant to the present. For Venturi, the cultural and historical background of an example was secondary.

The "Inclusion by Exclusion" of the example approach offers designers a flexible instrumentality, free from the constraints of typal logic or strict historical fidelity. At the same time, it draws on the familiarity and commonness of historical forms, enabling the creation of works that are both innovative and grounded in shared cultural recognition.

77 Agamben, "The Signature of All Things," p.24

78 Plato, "Statesman," 278c

CHARACTERISTIC 3 : INTELLECTUAL ENVIRONMENT

In this chapter, we move beyond the clarity and specificity of individual examples to explore the intellectual environment generated by utilizing multiple examples. This approach is commonly employed by sociologists to explain social phenomena, where individual examples serve as signals for identifying broader patterns and changes. The focus here is not on the individuality of a single example but on the collective intelligence that emerges from multiple examples.

The work of Pirro Ligorio, particularly his *Imago*, exemplifies this methodology in architecture. In *Imago*, Rome is portrayed as a composition of various historical relics, including domes, pyramids, obelisks, amphitheaters, and the Colosseum. However, the significance of Ligorio's work lies not merely in the arrangement of these diverse forms but in the perspective it conveys about the city of Rome. To fully grasp his viewpoint, it is essential to understand the historical context of Rome's significance within Europe.

Historically, and perhaps even today, Europe's emerging powers—spanning banking families, the nobility, and the bourgeoisie—were deeply captivated by the grandeur of ancient Rome. For these groups, the relics of Rome symbolized the cultural and political prestige of the Roman Empire and served as tools to legitimize their authority. These relics often became starting points for urban planning, linking the glories of the past to the present. This enduring practice of redeveloping Rome as a reflection of its historic grandeur was termed *Instauratio Urbis* (Restoration of the City).[79] Ligorio's *Imago* was conceived within this tradition, influencing later works such as Piranesi's *Antichità Romane* and Aldo Rossi's *Città Analoga*.

FIGURE 19 *Imago* by Pirro Ligorio

In summary, the examples used in *Imago* transcend technical or economic applications, such as zoning in contemporary urban planning. Instead, they construct an intellectual environment rooted in the latent memories and histories of the city. This framework offers a commonly applicable design methodology, capable of addressing broader cultural and philosophical questions.

While the "creation of an intellectual environment" through the example approach may appear more suited to expressing a philosophical perspective or worldview than to practical design tasks, it is not incompatible with pragmatism. J. N. L. Durand, successfully reconciled the creation of intellectual environments with practical design methodologies, a subject that will be explored in detail in Chapter 11.

79 For more details, refer to Pier Vittorio Aureli's "The Possibility of Absolute Architecture"

10
CHARACTERISTICS OF EXAMPLE APPROACH

VENTURI'S HISTORICAL BACKGROUND

When circumstances defy order, order should bend or break: anomalies and uncertainties give validity to architecture.[80]

ROBERT VENTURI

Robert Venturi was a key figure who actively employed examples as a design methodology. His approach is particularly evident in his seminal work, *Complexity and Contradiction in Architecture.* In this book, Venturi organizes his ideas in what can be described as an "architectural encyclopedia of examples," as illustrated by Figure 20 & 21, which depicts some pages from the book. To understand why Venturi adopted this approach, it is essential to consider the historical context of his time.

Following World War II, both Europe and the United States experienced a surge in new town developments to address the pressing need for large-scale housing. A prominent example is Levittown in the United States, created as part of welfare initiatives for returning war veterans. During this period, large-scale public projects like urban development were conducted under government planning, characterized by mechanized and systematic approaches. As a young architect, Venturi observed these developments and identified a unique opportunity. He recognized that the efficiency of

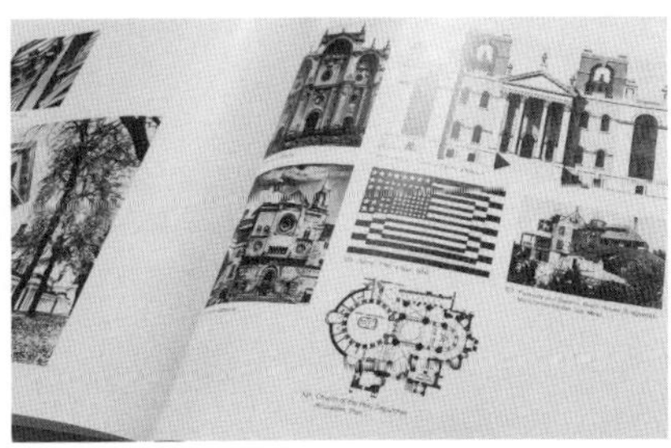

FIGURE 20 & 21 Pages from *Complexity and Contradiction in Architecture*

large-scale urban planning allowed architects to shift their focus toward the design of individual buildings, free from the constraints of overarching urban or political concerns. This realization profoundly influenced Venturi's architectural philosophy, driving his emphasis on the creative and value-free use of examples as a core methodology within the discipline.[81]

In this context, the literary critique method known as New Criticism[82] provided an ideal intellectual foundation for Robert Venturi's architectural approach. Venturi drew significant inspiration from the technique of *close reading*, a central practice in New Criticism. close reading involves evaluating a literary or artistic work by focusing exclusively on its internal forms and structures, disregarding external factors such as historical, social, or economic contexts. This method reflects a purely formalist perspective, in which the assessment of objects relies solely on their intrinsic qualities. Venturi applied this technique to architecture in *Complexity and Contradiction in Architecture.*[83] By adopting close reading as a design methodology, he liberated architectural examples from their historical contexts, repurposing them freely in his designs. For Venturi, the historical or cultural origins of these examples were secondary to their visual impact and communicative potential. What mattered was the symbolic and expressive power of the images they conveyed, enabling examples to become dynamic tools for architectural expression and dialogue, free from the constraints of their original meanings.

Another critical concept in Robert Venturi's architectural philosophy is mannerism, a term frequently mentioned in *Complexity and Contradiction in Architecture.* Mannerism refers to the artistic style that emerged after the High Renaissance and before the baroque period. Unlike the Renaissance, where form often served as an ideological or political tool, mannerism shifted its focus toward superficial ornamentation and the deliberate manipulation of form.

A quintessential example of mannerist architecture is the Casina di Pio (Figure 22), where an obsessive manipulation and invention of form overshadowed the common values of architecture, prioritizing visual spectacle instead. Venturi found this mannerist attitude—fixating exclusively on form—particularly useful for architects operating in contexts dominated by government-led, large-scale public developments and urban planning. For him, mannerism's emphasis on form offered a productive lens through which to rethink architecture's role within such rigid, top-down systems.

Venturi's *Complexity and Contradiction in Architecture* can thus be understood as a reinterpretation of the principles of close reading and mannerism, adapted to the challenges of modern architecture. He approached architectural history as a repository of examples to be used freely, deliberately stripping these examples of their ideological or cultural contexts in the design process. In Venturi's work, the focus is not on an overarching "framework" or the "formal structure" of type but on the relationships that highlight the individuality and interplay of each example or architectural element.

This perspective marked a significant shift from the broader universality of types to the specificity and communicative power of individual architectural elements. By doing so, Venturi offered a fresh approach to design in an era defined by overwhelming standardization, reinvigorating the discourse around architectural creativity and expression.

80 Venturi, "Complexity and Contradiction in Architecture," p.41

81 Refer to P.V. Aureli's AA School Lecture, Theory and Ethos: Towards a Common Architectural Language (Part 6)

82 New Criticism was a formalist movement in literary theory that dominated American literary criticism in the middle decades of the 20th century. It emphasized close reading, particularly of poetry, to discover how a work of literature functioned as a self-contained, self-referential aesthetic object. (https://en.wikipedia.org/wiki/New_Criticism#:~:text=New%20Criticism%20was%20a%20formalist,%2C%20self%2Dreferential%20aesthetic%20object.)

83 Refer to P.V. Aureli's AA School Lecture, Theory and Ethos: Towards a Common Architectural Language (Part 6)

FIGURE 22 Casa di Pio

FIGURE 23 Vanna Venturi House

INCLUSIVISM

As an architect I try to be guided not by habit but by a conscious sense of the past—by precedent, thoughtfully considered.[84]

ROBERT VENTURI

As discussed in the previous chapter, Robert Venturi's architectural philosophy embraced examples as essential materials for design. This methodology was also employed by other architects and theorists of the 1960s, including Denise Scott Brown, Charles Moore, and Vincent Scully. Collectively, this approach became known as Inclusivism.[85] For Venturi, historical examples functioned as ready-made objects, detached from their original social and cultural contexts and perpetually available for reinterpretation. The intrigue of this process lies in the exceptional ways these examples are reassembled to address contemporary needs or to create compositions unimaginable in their original contexts. In this sense, Venturi's architecture can be understood as a collage, where diverse historical references are uniquely combined and preserved within a single architectural drawing. Through this approach, the examples Venturi employed became liberated from the continuity of history, existing instead in an eternal "present" shaped by his creative vision. This exemplifies how the inclusivist approach transformed historical references into flexible tools for modern architectural expression, redefining their meanings in innovative and contextually relevant ways.

Interpreting Venturi's rejection of historical "continuity" as a dismissal of architectural history itself—akin to the stance of some modernist architects—would be a profound misunderstanding. Paradoxically, for Venturi, architectural history was the most vital repository of knowledge and form. By transferring historical examples into the present, he engaged in what Manfredo Tafuri termed the "actualization of history." For Venturi, this process of integrating historical examples into contemporary design was not about discarding history but about reinterpreting it to make it relevant and meaningful for current needs. His approach illustrated how the past could serve as a dynamic and living resource, rather than a restrictive framework, enabling an architecture that was simultaneously grounded in historical awareness and oriented toward the future.

Another significant effect of inclusivism on Venturi's architecture is the absence of discussions about formal structure or overarching frameworks, which are central to type.[86] In Venturi's work, emphasis shifts away from the logical and syntactic coherence of a unified whole. Instead, his architecture is distinctly semantic, prioritizing the individuality and communicative power of its components. This approach stands in sharp contrast to the work of his contemporary, Peter Eisenman.

As illustrated in Figure 24, Eisenman's architectural process resembles filmmaking. He begins with a generic form and rigorously controls the design process according to self-defined principles. If the desired outcome is not achieved, Eisenman does not compromise but revises the intermediate steps, effectively "editing" the design process to craft a scenario that produces the intended result. His architecture is thus syntactic, adhering strictly to continuity and the progression of its design logic.

Venturi, by contrast, employs a methodology akin to montage in cinema or collage in painting. His philosophy is captured in his statement: "I like elements which are hybrid rather than 'pure,' compromising rather than 'clean,' distorted rather than 'straightforward,' ambiguous rather than 'articulated,' perverse as well as impersonal, boring as well as 'interesting,' conventional rather than 'designed,' accommodating rather than excluding, redundant rather than simple, vestigial as well as innovating, inconsistent and equivocal rather than direct and clear."[87]

In summary, Venturi applied the principles of "moving from particular to particular," as discussed in Characteristic 1 of the example approach, along with the "inclusion by exclusion nature of examples" described in Characteristic 2. The result is an inclusivist architecture that respects history while feeling simultaneously innovative and common. Venturi's method demonstrates how historical references and diverse examples can be creatively integrated to produce architecture bridges the past and present in unexpected ways.

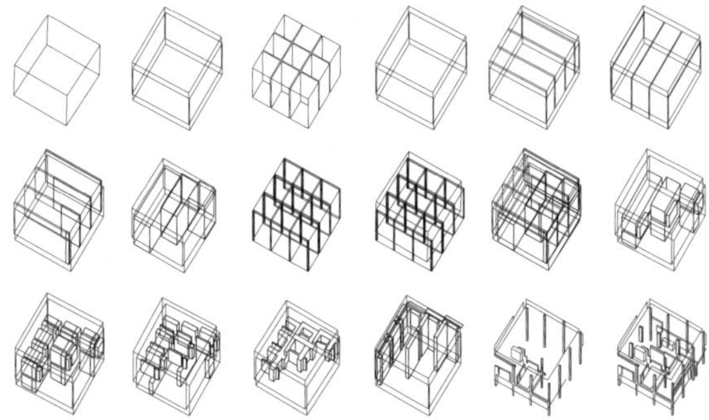

FIGURE 24 Process diagram of House 2 by Peter Eisenman

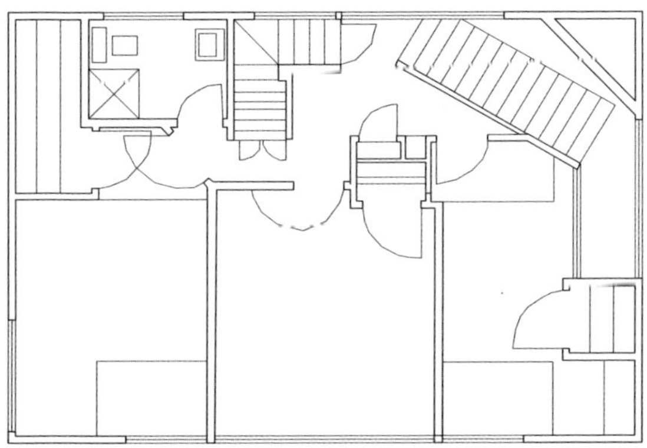

FIGURE 25 Trubek House

84 Venturi, "Complexity and Contradiction in Architecture," p.13

85 Cohen, "Physical Context / Cultural Context: Including it all, OPPOSITIONS Reader 1973-1984," p.66

86 Cohen, "Physical Context / Cultural Context: Including it all, OPPOSITIONS Reader 1973-1984," p.66

87 Venturi, "Complexity and Contradiction in Architecture," p.16

EXAMPLES ARE IMAGES

It's not that the past casts its light on what is present, or what is present its light on the past; rather, the image is that wherein what has been comes together in a flash with the now to form a constellation. In other words, the image is dialectics at a standstill.[88]

WALTER BENJAMIN

Complexity and Contradiction in Architecture (1966) and *Learning from Las Vegas* (1972) vividly illustrate the evolution of Robert Venturi's architectural philosophy. In particular, *Learning from Las Vegas* expands upon several architectural values initially explored in *Complexity and Contradiction*, with a notable focus on the concepts of "image" and "message."

In this context, image and message are neither abstract nor hidden ideas. Venturi and Denise Scott Brown argue in *Learning from Las Vegas* that architects should prioritize the visible image of a building and the message it conveys, rather than concentrating solely on form or the logic of the design process.[89] This perspective represents a shift from valuing "what is known"—the underlying logic or structure of a design—to valuing "what is seen"—the visual and symbolic impact of architecture.[90]

This symbolist approach emphasizes the significance of what a building or architectural element symbolizes over its historical or spatial context. For Venturi and Scott Brown, the communicative power of architecture lies in its ability to project clear and accessible images and messages, making these elements central to their design philosophy. By challenging traditional architectural priorities, they elevate the importance of visual and symbolic clarity in the built environment, reshaping how architecture engages with its audience.

To understand the emphasis on image in architecture, it is helpful to examine its historical development. Since the Renaissance, the relationship between "inside and outside" has been a central concern in Western architecture. As discussed in Chapter 2, the facade—the most visible part of a building that interacts with the city and the public—was not merely an exterior or decorative surface. It functioned as a medium to communicate moral and political values, serving as an image that conveyed meaning.

In contrast, modernist architecture rejected this dualism between inside and outside. Rooted in an ethical imperative, modernism insisted that facades should transparently reveal the interior, reducing the external appearance to a direct expression of the internal structure and spatial organization.

Venturi and Denise Scott Brown rejected this modernist fixation on transparency. For them, the facade was an independent element, separate from other aspects of the building, such as form or structure. They regarded the facade as a manipulable image or language that architects could design freely. This perspective resonates with the principles of mannerism discussed in the previous chapter, where the deliberate manipulation of forms takes precedence.

In this context, the concept of the "Decorated Shed," introduced in *Learning from Las Vegas*, exemplifies their approach to architecture as an effective means of communication. For Venturi and Scott Brown, "decoration" was not merely ornamental but symbolic—symbols were images that conveyed a building's meaning. As such, they argued that the most efficient way for architecture to communicate its content was not through form or structure but through facades that operated independently of spatial or structural constraints.

Their perspective on the facade as an image is succinctly encapsulated in *Learning from Las Vegas*, where they underscore their commitment to liberating the facade from modernist dogma and using it as a powerful tool for architectural communication.

"We shall emphasize image—image over process or form—in asserting that architecture depends on its perception and creation on past experience and emotional association and that these symbolic and representational elements may often be contradictory to the form, structure, and program with which they combine in the same building."[91]

In architecture, images serve as a medium with minimal potential for misinterpretation or ambiguity, making the facade one of the most effective tools for communication. This characteristic aligns closely with the specificity of examples. The examples Venturi employs can be understood as images chosen for their capacity to facilitate immediate and efficient communication.

In summary, across his two major works, Venturi treats examples—whether in plan or facade—as images, liberating them from the constraints of typal structures and enabling their unrestricted combination. His example approach frees architectural design from the burden of type's historicity and continuity while leveraging the commonness inherent in familiar, pre-existing images.

By reassembling familiar images in innovative ways, as Venturi does, architects can create a new form of commonness that resonates with contemporary eras and cultures. This process of recombining the familiar to address present-day contexts represents one of the most significant contributions architects can make toward achieving common architecture.

Communication dominates space as an element in architecture.[92]

FROM *LEARNING FROM LAS VEGAS*

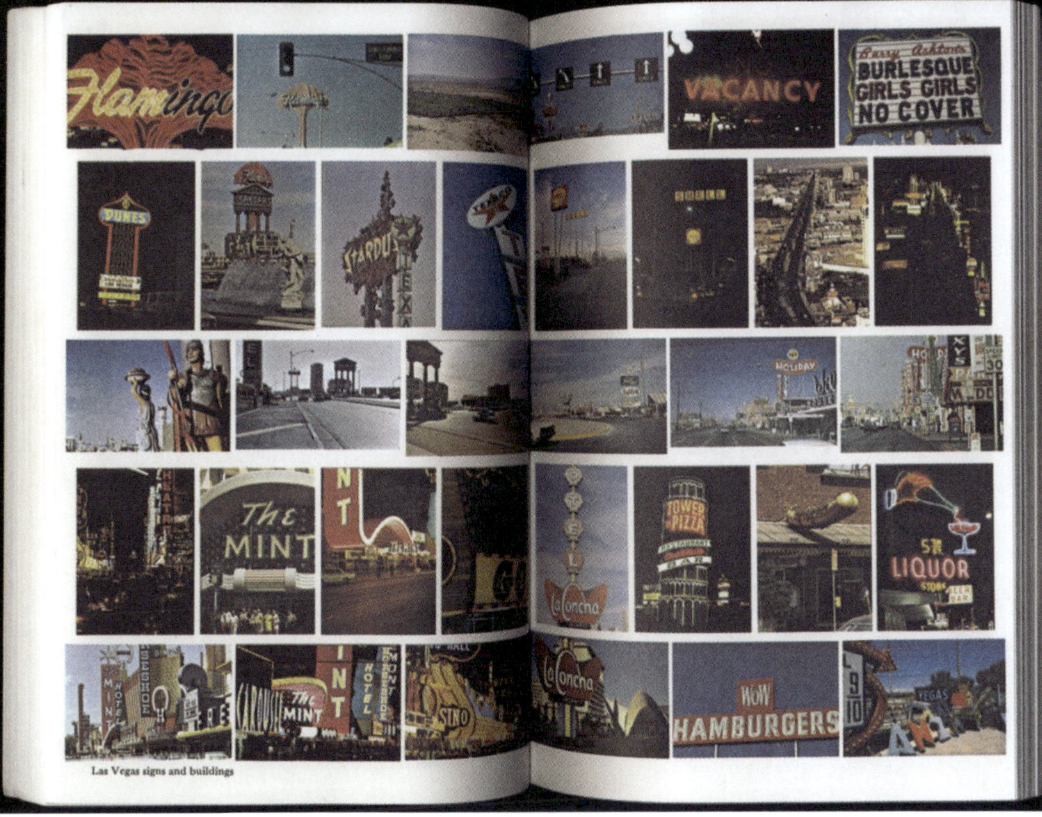

FIGURE 26 Pages from *Learning From The Las Vegas*

88 Benjamin, "Arcades Project," p.462

89 Scott-Brown, Venturi, Izenour, "Learning from Las Vegas," p.87

90 Jacoby, "The Reasoning of Architecture", p.7295 Venturi, "Complexity and Contradiction in Architecture," p.16

91 Scott-Brown, "Venturi, Izenour, Learning from Las Vegas," p.87

92 Scott-Brown, "Venturi, Izenour, Learning from Las Vegas," p.8

11

J.N.L. DURAND'S EXAMPLE APPROACH

J.N.L. DURAND'S PRECEDENTS

In a similar vein as anatomy, in Durand's method, buildings were dissected, opened and decomposed in their many parts, treated as forensic evidence in which each part was the object of analysis.[93]

ALEJANDRA CELEDON

Jean Nicolas Louis Durand, a French architect and educator, approached architecture from a scientific and positivist perspective, laying the intellectual groundwork for modern architecture. His lectures at the École de Polytechnique were compiled into his seminal work, *Précis Des Leçons* D'architecture, which systematically dissects architecture into quantifiable components. As shown in Figure 27, Durand deconstructed buildings

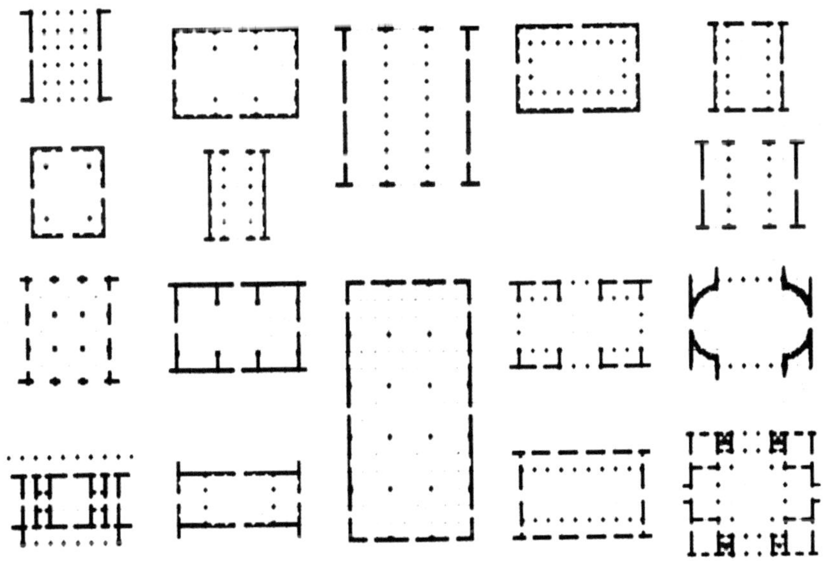

FIGURE 27 Plate from *Précis Des Leçons*, showcasing vestibule examples

into individual elements, all derived from existing architectural examples. Through these examples, he introduced an efficient, assembly like design methodology, akin to building with Lego blocks.

However, before architecture could be "deconstructed" and "recombined," it required rigorous comparison and analysis. The critical aspect of Durand's methodology was not the static diagrams of dissected examples but the intellectual environment he created by comparing and analyzing architectural history across different cultures and eras. In this context, his earlier work, *Recueil et Parallèle* (1801), served as an essential precursor to *Précis Des Leçons D'architecture*. This earlier volume presented a vast collection of architectural examples categorized by function. For instance, Figure 28 depicts temples from various regions and cultures, all presented at the same scale, enabling Durand to identify diverse solutions for each function.

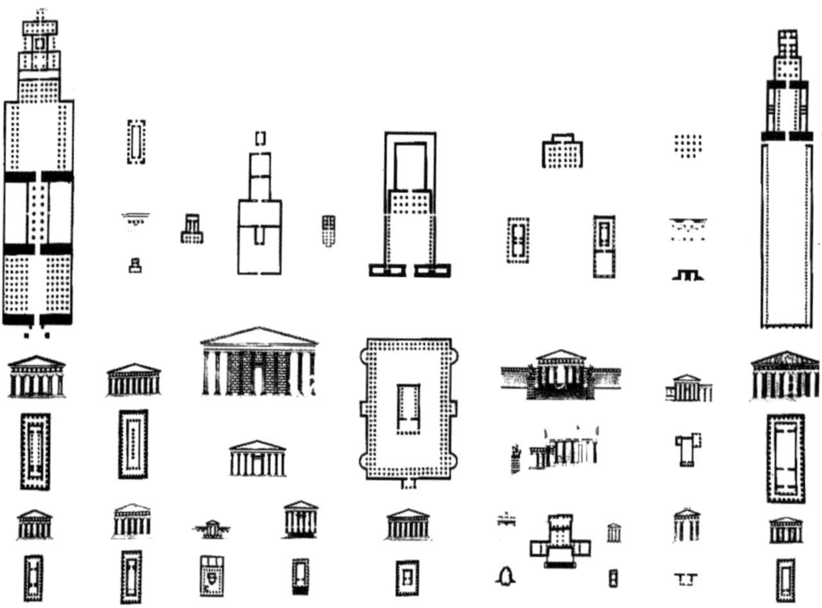

FIGURE 28 Plate from *Précis Des Leçons*, showcasing vestibule examples

This extensive data allowed Durand to confidently deconstruct and recombine architectural elements. The process of "deconstruction and recombination" represents the most significant outcome of his case studies.

Durand's case studies diverge from the typical role of precedent studies in architectural practice. Architects often begin the design process by examining precedents to identify potential solutions for a given program. However, this process is frequently influenced by personal taste or intuition, as architects are drawn to specific forms or images. While this approach is effective for building upon proven examples, it has inherent limitations: intuitive judgment can skew the selection of examples. Experience may improve the quality of these decisions, but history shows that experience alone does not guarantee better outcomes. Therefore, "intuitive decision from experience" cannot reliably determine the "first move" in the design process or ensure the best choice of precedent.

In this context, Durand's case studies illustrate how examples can be employed to construct an intellectual environment for logical deconstruction and recombination. This method allowed Durand to present his architectural philosophy systematically and logically, offering a strategy to transcend the limitations of intuition-based design and enabling a more rigorous, objective approach to architectural exploration.

93 Celedon, "Plan as Eidos," p.5

DURAND'S HISTORICAL BACKGROUND

To fully understand Durand's modular architecture, we must examine the late 18th-century context in which he worked. For over a millennium, from Rome through the Renaissance, Western architecture was centered in Italy, a fragmented collection of city-states ruled by noble families and guilds. By the 18th century, however, the rise of the nation-state shifted architectural dominance to France. The nation-state's primary challenge was governing an entire country rather than a single city. Architecture became a crucial tool in this process, shaping public space and reinforcing centralized power. Another consequence of this political transformation was secularization—transcendental values like religion lost influence, replaced by economy and market logic tied to the rise of the bourgeoisie.[94]

The link between the nation-state and economy becomes clear when we examine the etymology of the word economy. Derived from the Greek *oikos*, meaning "house" or "household management," the original meaning of economy was not solely about money but about systems of organization and control. For a nation-state to function, it required an efficient system to manage its complex society, and economic principles became an essential tool for this. The most universal medium of economic exchange was, of course, money.

Traditionally, architects designed buildings for kings, churches, and other centers of power, expressing their political and ideological authority. However, with the emergence of schools, courts, markets, and public housing developments, architecture became a tool of management, prioritized for economic efficiency rather than ideological representation.[95] In this transition, classical architecture lost its role as a symbol of political and ideological power, becoming a detached, hollow ideal.

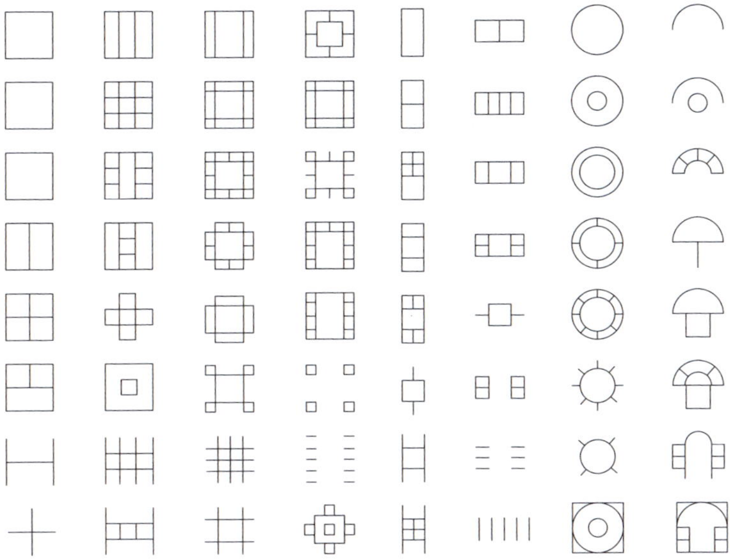

FIGURE 29 Plate from *Précis Des Leçons*, showing examples of "compositions"'

As societies moved away from religious influences, a positivist attitude—demanding empirical, rational approaches—became dominant across all disciplines, including architecture. France, at the heart of these changes before and after the Revolution, became the perfect setting for Durand's approach. Naturally, he adopted a positivist, rational, and economic stance toward architecture. His response was the deconstruction and recombination of countless architectural examples, as discussed in the previous chapter. However, Durand's method differs significantly from Venturi's approach. In the next chapter, we will explore Durand's architectural philosophy in greater detail to examine these distinctions.

94 Refer to Pier Vittorio Aureli's AA School Lecture: Theory and Ethos: Towards a Common Architectural Language Part 4 (2012)

95 Picon, "Poetry of Art" to *Method: The Theory of Jean-Nicolas-Louis Durand*, p.16

DURAND'S INTELLECTUAL ENVIRONMENT: "COMPOSITION"

The typology that Durand has in mind is not a catalog of immediately applicable solutions but a system of classifications that makes it possible to familiarize oneself with the various problems that may turn up in practice.[96]

ANTOINE PICON

As previously discussed, the rise of the nation-state led to the secularization of society. In this transformation, absolute values such as "God" or "Nature" were gradually replaced by economy and market logic. Within this broader shift in value systems, the concept of "taste" emerged as a justification for personal fantasy and consumerism.[97] Jean Nicolas Louis Durand sought to replace this subjective notion of taste with a common standard of architectural value, which he identified in the concept of composition.

Composition, a central theme in *Précis Des Leçons D'architecture*, encapsulates Durand's architectural philosophy. It is defined through the interplay of two fundamental questions: "What" constitutes the whole? This question addresses the individual units that form the composition. "How" is the whole composed? This question focuses on the method of assembling those units.[98] The most intriguing aspect of composition is the clear separation it establishes between the whole and its parts. This separation requires decision-making based on specific value criteria, and for Durand, the "fact" that certain historical examples had already proven their value became this criterion. In other words, for Durand, analyzing historical examples and extracting the necessary components was itself a common architectural value that could replace personal taste.

Another key aspect of separation is analysis. Scientists and engineers analyze complex phenomena step by step, identifying problems, arranging them in sequence, and efficiently solving them. Durand applied this same analytical approach to architecture. By systematically studying architectural elements and their compositional methods, he aimed to create a more efficient design process. In this way, he introduced the scientific method into architecture, establishing a design methodology that could be universally accepted in modern society.[99]

In summary, Durand moved beyond the reproduction of classical architecture and introduced "positivist architecture," which relied on the rational assembly of parts derived from historical precedents. For him, the most critical architectural principle was composition, or the most rational and efficient method of combining elements. However, if composition is simply a matter of assembling historical examples to create an intellectual framework, how does it differ from the exemplary approach used by Pirro Ligorio's *Imago* or Piranesi's Campo Marzio, as discussed in Chapter 9? Durand's key distinction lies in his use of the axis (Axis) and grid (Grid). Figure 30 illustrates how Durand employs these tools: The axis serves as the spatial center, organizing the composition. The grid acts as a guideline for the efficient arrangement of columns and walls.

For Durand, the axis and grid function as an architectural autopilot, providing efficiency and economic logic in the method of assembling examples. This is where Durand fundamentally differs from Ligorio or Piranesi, whose approaches were more pictorial and symbolic.

By incorporating axes and grids, Durand successfully integrated economic rationality and scientific thinking into architecture, aligning with the demands of a secularized society that prioritized economic value and rationality.

The intellectual foundation that allowed Durand to use the axis and grid was his meticulous process of analyzing, deconstructing, and recom-

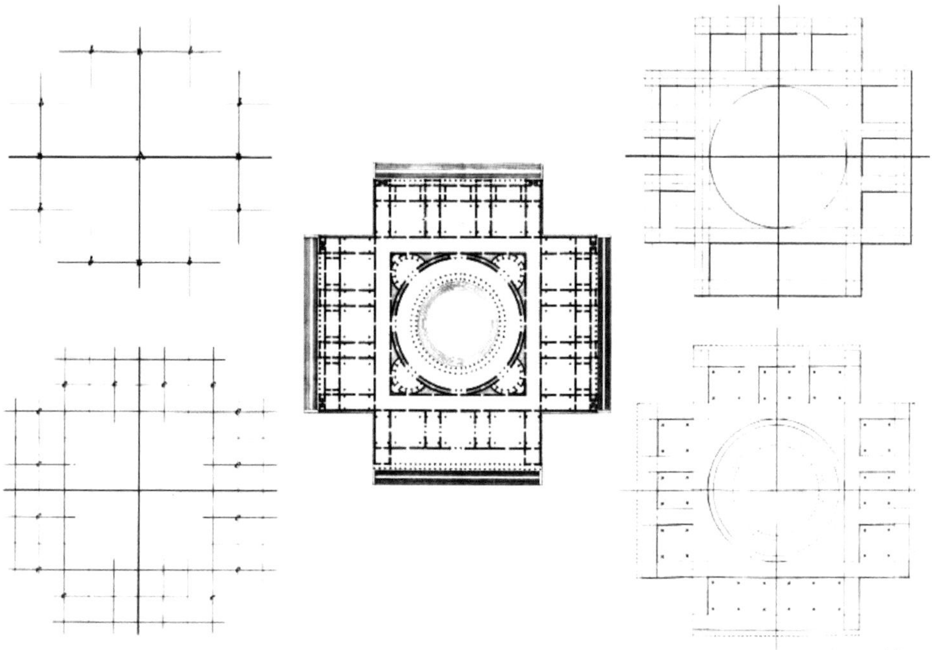

FIGURE 30 "Procedure to be followed in the composition of whatever building" from *Précis Des Leçons.* This plate illustrates his use of grids and axes to optimize design efficiency

posing historical examples. While his diagrams and methods may appear dry and mechanical, they achieve clarity and familiarity through historical precedent, making them culturally and socially significant.

Understanding the historical context of Durand's work reveals that his architecture cannot be dismissed as merely mechanical. Instead, it represents a meaningful attempt to reconcile rational design with the social, economic, and intellectual shifts of his time.

The typology that Durand has in mind is not a catalog of immediately applicable solutions but a system of classifications that makes it possible to familiarize oneself with the various problems that may turn up in practice.[100]

ANTOINE PICON

96 Picon, "Poetry of Art to Method: The Theory of Jean Nicolas Louis Durand," p.45
97 Vidler, "The Idea of Type," p.95-97
98 Aurell, "The Possibility of Absolute Architecture," p.165
99 Picon, "*Poetry of Art*" *to Method: The Theory of Jean-Nicolas-Louis Durand*, p.42
100 Celedon, "Plan as Eidos", p.4

12
INCEPTION OF DESIGN: TYPOLOGICAL AND EXAMPLE APPROACH

So far, we have explored how the concepts of "types" and "examples" shape architectural thinking and design methodology. The main reason for writing on this topic was to provide a more rational and common framework for explaining the design process, which is often influenced by the subjective preferences of architects or clients. I believed that if the design process could be explained based on common logic, it would enable healthier public discussions on architecture.

To achieve this vision of "common architecture," three key challenges had to be addressed: 1. Ensuring that the first move in the design process, often seen as arbitrary, could be explained rationally; 2. Establishing a consistent and logical framework for developing that first move; 3. Integrating all of this into an architectural concept that allows for common communication.

Architectural and art theorist Anthony Vidler categorized three types of first moves in architectural design.[101]

First, the "Primitive Hut" theory by Abbé Laugier, a French clergyman, who saw nature as the origin of architecture. During his time, nature was understood as God's divine order, represented through proportion, geometry, and fundamental principles. Second, the idea that industrial context dictates the starting point of architecture, where materials, construction technologies, and economic systems shape architectural decisions. Le Corbusier's Maison Dom-ino represents this approach, emphasizing a clear and rational structural framework. Third, the perspective, championed by architects like Aldo Rossi, that sees the urban environment as a repository of architectural forms, using it as the basis for design.

All three approaches provided rational justifications for the first move in architectural design and were framed within common logic. However, a significant limitation of these theories was the arbitrariness in how they were translated into built form. For example, in Le Corbusier's Ville

FIGURE 31 Primitive Hut by Laugier

Contemporaine (a city for three million), the clarity and simplicity of Maison Dom-ino disappear, replaced by a collection of diverse typologies and examples, reflecting personal choices rather than pure rationality. Similarly, in Aldo Rossi's work, after his early projects, his architecture gradually became dominated by a highly subjective style, making it difficult to discern the rationalist passion he originally advocated.[102]

Despite the arbitrariness in achieving common architecture, the complementarity of typological and example approaches is essential to addressing the three challenges mentioned earlier.

The typological approach provides a broad and abstract formal structure that is socially and culturally appropriate as the starting point in architectural design. The example approach gives specificity to the typological structure, situating it within a familiar knowledge system. Lastly, the historicity of both

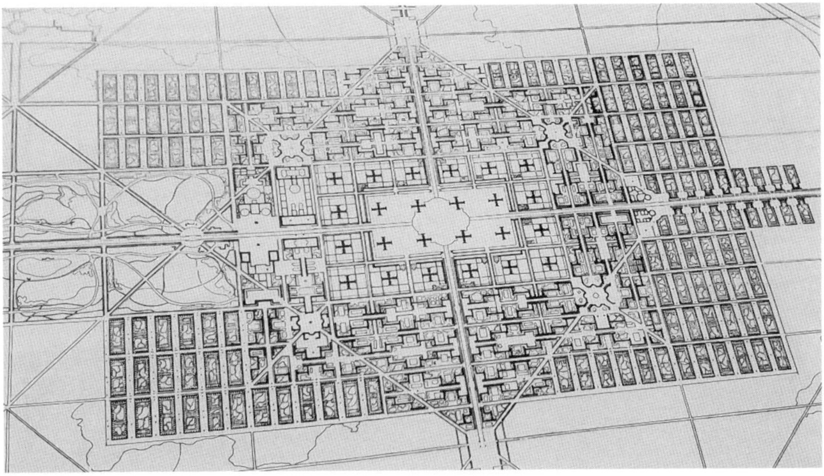

FIGURE 32 Le Corbusier's Ville Contemporaine

types and examples ensures that the entire process can be communicated universally.

For these reasons, types and examples have consistently held enduring value as foundational elements in architectural design, and they will continue to do so. Their ability to balance abstraction and specificity while ensuring cultural relevance and effective communication makes them indispensable tools for creating common architecture.

Architectural knowledge ought to be general and accessible as an art that brings such great and manifold benefits to humanity and to society when well understood.[103]

SAM JACOBY

101 Vidler, "Third Typology," p.13, *Oppositions Reader*
102 Refer to P.V.Aureli, AA School Lecture, 2012, *Theory and Ethos: Towards a Common Architectural Language*, Part6
103 Jacoby, "The Reasoning of Architecture," p.78

PHILOSOPHICAL ASPECT OF ARCHITECTURE

Ludwig Feuerbach stated that the "philosophical aspect" of any discipline means its "potential for development." From this perspective, the persistent divide between theory and practice in architecture is a regrettable reality. Theory is often dismissed by practitioners as detached from reality, while practitioners are criticized by academics for merely producing designs that cater to market demands. However, if architects lack a theoretical or historical foundation in architecture, they have no clear criteria for distinguishing between good and bad design. Without such criteria, architects risk becoming mere service providers. Conversely, possessing philosophical knowledge but retreating into idealistic concepts while criticizing the practical realities of architecture is also an empty stance.

Etymologically, "theory" means "perspective." In this sense, concepts like "philosophical aspect" or "theory" are not difficult but rather represent the potential for growth and the viewpoints individuals bring to their work. Thus, we are all philosophers and theorists. However, architecture is increasingly losing its philosophical passion, swept away by new technologies and market forces. As a result, architects today struggle to sustain their careers, let alone challenge this trend.

Despite this, Aldo Rossi once said, "The creation of a design theory is the first objective of an architectural school for all other types of research. A design theory is the most important and creative moment of every architecture." In this light, viewing theory merely as a tool for post-rationalizing design decisions is a significant misunderstanding and writing is arguably a more common medium than design itself for communicating architectural knowledge.

Architecture is not simply "design"—therefore, architectural study extends beyond designing and constructing buildings; it is the construction of thought about the spaces and environments we inhabit. These constructed thoughts reveal the "philosophical aspects" of our surroundings—their potential for development—and consequently, the most critical task for architects is the craft of constructing ideas.

BIBLIOGRAPHY

- AGAMBEN, GIORGIO. *THE SIGNATURE OF ALL THINGS: ON METHOD.* TRANSLATED BY LUCA D'ISANTO AND KEVIN ATTELL. NEW YORK: ZONE BOOKS, 2009.
- ALBERTI, LEON BATTISTA. *ON THE ART OF BUILDING IN TEN BOOKS.* TRANSLATED BY JOSEPH RYKWERT, NEIL LEACH, AND ROBERT TAVERNOR. CAMBRIDGE, MA: MIT PRESS, 1988.
- ARGAN, GIULIO CARLO. "*ON THE TYPOLOGY OF ARCHITECTURE.*" ARCHITECTURAL DESIGN 33, NO. 12 (1963): 564–576.
- ARISTOTLE. *PRIOR ANALYTICS.* TRANSLATED BY ROBIN SMITH. INDIANAPOLIS: HACKETT PUBLISHING COMPANY, 1989.
- AURELI, PIER VITTORIO. *THE POSSIBILITY OF ABSOLUTE ARCHITECTURE.* CAMBRIDGE, MA: MIT PRESS, 2011.
- AURELI, PIER VITTORIO. "*LIFE ABSTRACTED: NOTES ON THE FLOOR PLAN.*" E-FLUX ARCHITECTURE, 2018. HTTPS://WWW.E-FLUX.COM/ARCHITECTURE/REPRESENTATION/159199/LIFE-ABSTRACTED-NOTES-ON-THE-FLOOR-PLAN/
- AURELI, PIER VITTORIO. "*APPROPRIATION, SUBDIVISION, ABSTRACTION: A POLITICAL HISTORY OF THE URBAN GRID.*" LOG 44 (FALL 2018): 139–167.
- BENJAMIN, WALTER. *THE ARCADES PROJECT.* TRANSLATED BY HOWARD EILAND AND KEVIN MCLAUGHLIN. CAMBRIDGE, MA: BELKNAP PRESS OF HARVARD UNIVERSITY PRESS, 1999.
- CARL, PETER. "*TYPE, FIELD, CULTURE, PRAXIS.*" IN TYPOLOGICAL URBANISM: PROJECTIVE CITIES, EDITED BY CHRISTOPHER C.M. LEE AND SAM JACOBY, 38–45. ARCHITECTURAL DESIGN 81, NO. 1 (2011): 38–45. HTTPS://DOI.ORG/10.1002/AD.1187.
- CELEDÓN, ALEJANDRA. "*FOOTPRINTS.*" ARQ 92 (2016): 30–39. HTTPS://WWW.SCIELO.CL/SCIELO.PHP?PID=S0717-69962016000200009.
- CELEDÓN, ALEJANDRA. "*THE PLAN AS EIDOS: BRAMANTE'S HALF-DRAWING AND DURAND'S MARCHE.*" IN PROCEEDINGS OF THE THIRD INTERNATIONAL MEETING OF THE EUROPEAN ARCHITECTURAL HISTORY NETWORK (EAHN), TURIN, ITALY, JUNE 19–21, 2014.
- COHEN, STUART. "*PHYSICAL CONTEXT/CULTURAL CONTEXT: INCLUDING IT ALL.*" OPPOSITIONS 2 (1974): 1–40.
- COLQUHOUN, ALAN. "*TYPOLOGY AND DESIGN METHOD.*" PERSPECTA 12 (1969): 71–74. HTTPS://DOI.ORG/10.2307/1566943.
- DURAND, JEAN-NICOLAS-LOUIS. *PRÉCIS OF THE LECTURES ON ARCHITECTURE: WITH GRAPHIC PORTION OF THE LECTURES ON ARCHITECTURE.* TRANSLATED BY DAVID BRITT. INTRODUCTION BY ANTOINE PICON. LOS ANGELES: GETTY RESEARCH INSTITUTE, 2000.
- EISENMAN, PETER. THE FORMAL BASIS OF MODERN ARCHITECTURE. NEW YORK: LARS MÜLLER PUBLISHERS, 2006. ORIGINALLY PUBLISHED IN 1963
- NIGEL GORING-MORRIS AND ANNA BELFER-COHEN, "*A ROOF OVER ONE'S HEAD: DEVELOPMENTS IN NEAR EASTERN RESIDENTIAL ARCHITECTURE ACROSS THE EPIPALAEOLITHIC–NEOLITHIC TRANSITION,*" IN THE NEOLITHIC DEMOGRAPHIC TRANSITION AND ITS CONSEQUENCES, ED. JEAN-PIERRE BOCQUET-APPEL AND OFER BAR-YOSEF (DORDRECHT: SPRINGER, 2008), 239–286, HTTPS://DOI.ORG/10.1007/978-1-4020-8539-0_10.
- HARRIS, STEVEN E. "*SOVIET MASS HOUSING AND THE COMMUNIST WAY OF LIFE." IN EVERYDAY LIFE IN RUSSIA PAST AND PRESENT,* EDITED BY CHOI CHATTERJEE, DAVID L. RANSEL, MARY CAVENDER, AND KAREN PETRONE, 181–204. BLOOMINGTON: INDIANA UNIVERSITY PRESS, 2015.
- JACOBY, SAM. *THE REASONING OF ARCHITECTURE: TYPE AND THE PROBLEM OF HISTORICITY.* PHD DISS., TECHNISCHE UNIVERSITÄT BERLIN, 2013.
- KUBLER, GEORGE. *THE SHAPE OF TIME: REMARKS ON THE HISTORY OF THINGS.* NEW HAVEN, CT: YALE UNIVERSITY PRESS, 1962
- LATHOURI, MARINA. "*THE CITY AS A PROJECT: TYPES, TYPICAL OBJECTS AND TYPOLOGIES.*" IN TYPOLOGICAL URBANISM: PROJECTIVE CITIES, EDITED BY CHRISTOPHER C.M. LEE AND SAM JACOBY, 24–31. ARCHITECTURAL DESIGN 81, NO. 1 (2011): 24–31.

- LEE, CHRISTOPHER C.M. "*TYPE.*" IN TYPOLOGICAL URBANISM: PROJECTIVE CITIES, EDITED BY CHRISTOPHER C.M. LEE AND SAM JACOBY, 14–23. ARCHITECTURAL DESIGN 81, NO. 1 (2011): 14–23.
- LOBSINGER, MARY LOUISE. "*THAT OBSCURE OBJECT OF DESIRE: AUTOBIOGRAPHY AND REPETITION IN THE WORK OF ALDO ROSSI.*" GREY ROOM, NO. 8 (2002): 38–61
- MARX, KARL. *GRUNDRISSE: FOUNDATIONS OF THE CRITIQUE OF POLITICAL ECONOMY (ROUGH DRAFT).* TRANSLATED BY MARTIN NICOLAUS. LONDON: PENGUIN BOOKS, 1973
- MAZZA, LUIGI. "*PLAN AND CONSTITUTION: ARISTOTLE'S HIPPODAMUS.*" TOWN PLANNING REVIEW 80, NO. 2 (2009): 113–141
- MCEWEN, INDRA KAGIS. *VITRUVIUS: WRITING THE BODY OF ARCHITECTURE.* CAMBRIDGE, MA: MIT PRESS, 2003.
- MONEO, RAFAEL. "*ON TYPOLOGY.*" OPPOSITIONS 13 (1978): 23–45.
- MORLEY, NEVILLE. "*CITIES IN CONTEXT: URBAN SYSTEMS IN ROMAN ITALY.*" IN ROMAN URBANISM: BEYOND THE CONSUMER CITY, EDITED BY HELEN PARKINS, 42–58. LONDON: ROUTLEDGE, 1997.
- PICON, PERRAULT, CLAUDE. *ORDONNANCE DES CINQ ESPÈCES DE COLONNES SELON LA MÉTHODE DES ANCIENS.* PARIS: JEAN-BAPTISTE COIGNARD, 1683.
- PICON, ANTOINE. "*FROM 'POETRY OF ART' TO METHOD: THE THEORY OF JEAN-NICOLAS-LOUIS DURAND.*" IN PRÉCIS OF THE LECTURES ON ARCHITECTURE, BY JEAN-NICOLAS-LOUIS DURAND, TRANSLATED BY DAVID BRITT, 1–72. LOS ANGELES: GETTY RESEARCH INSTITUTE, 2000.
- PLATO. *STATESMAN.* 287 B.C. TRANSLATED BY C.J. ROWE. CAMBRIDGE: CAMBRIDGE UNIVERSITY PRESS, 1995.
- QUATREMÈRE DE QUINCY, ANTOINE-CHRYSOSTOME. *AN ESSAY ON THE NATURE, THE END, AND THE MEANS OF IMITATION IN THE FINE ARTS.* TRANSLATED BY J.C. KENT. LONDON: SMITH, ELDER AND CO., 1837. HTTPS://ARCHIVE.ORG/DETAILS/ANESSAYONNATURE00CGOOG.
- QUATREMÈRE DE QUINCY, ANTOINE-CHRYSOSTOME. *DICTIONNAIRE HISTORIQUE D'ARCHITECTURE: COMPRENANT DANS SON PLAN LES NOTIONS HISTORIQUES, DESCRIPTIVES, ARCHÉOLOGIQUES, BIOGRAPHIQUES, THÉORIQUES, DIDACTIQUES ET PRATIQUES DE CET ART.* PARIS: LECLERE, 1832.
- QUATREMÈRE DE QUINCY, ANTOINE-CHRYSOSTOME. *ENCYCLOPÉDIE MÉTHODIQUE: ARCHITECTURE, VOL. 3, PT. 2.* PARIS: MME. VEUVE AGASSE, 1825
- ROSSI, ALDO. *THE ARCHITECTURE OF THE CITY.* TRANSLATED BY DIANEGHIRARDO AND JOAN OCKMAN. CAMBRIDGE, MA: MIT PRESS, 1982.
- ROSSI, ALDO. "*ARCHITECTURE FOR MUSEUMS.*" IN ALDO ROSSI: SELECTED WRITINGS AND PROJECTS, EDITED BY JOHN O'REGAN, 14 25. LONDON: ARCHITECTURAL DESIGN; DUBLIN: GANDON EDITIONS, 1983.
- ROSSI, ALDO. *A SCIENTIFIC AUTOBIOGRAPHY.* TRANSLATED BY LAWRENCE VENUTI. CAMBRIDGE, MA: MIT PRESS, 1981.
- ROWE, PETER G. "*A PRIORI KNOWLEDGE AND HEURISTIC REASONING IN ARCHITECTURAL DESIGN.*" JOURNAL OF ARCHITECTURAL EDUCATION 36, NO. 1 (1982): 18–23.
- SEMPER, "*SCIENCE, INDUSTRY AND ART,*" 1852
- VENTURI, ROBERT. *COMPLEXITY AND CONTRADICTION IN ARCHITECTURE.* NEW YORK: MUSEUM OF MODERN ART, 1966.
- VENTURI, ROBERT, DENISE SCOTT BROWN, AND STEVEN IZENOUR. *LEARNING FROM LAS VEGAS: THE FORGOTTEN SYMBOLISM OF ARCHITECTURAL FORM.* CAMBRIDGE, MA: MIT PRESS, 1972.
- VERNANT, JEAN-PIERRE. *MYTH AND THOUGHT AMONG THE GREEKS.* TRANSLATED BY JANET LLOYD AND JEFF FORT. NEW YORK: ZONE BOOKS, 2006
- VIDLER, ANTHONY. "*THE THIRD TYPOLOGY.*" OPPOSITIONS 7 (1976): 1–4.
- VITRUVIUS, *DE ARCHITECTURA*, TRANS. MORRIS HICKY MORGAN (NEW YORK: DOVER PUBLICATIONS, 1960), ORIGINALLY PUBLISHED IN 1914.
- 박인석. *아파트: 한국 사회.* 서울: 한겨레출판, 2013.
- 박철수. *거주 박물지.* 서울: 집, 2015
- 박철수. *아파트: 공적 냉소와 사적 정열이 지배하는 사회.* 서울: 집, 2013.
- 황두진. *무지개떡 건축.* 서울: 메디치미디어, 2015.

IMAGES

FIGURE1: HTTPS://EN.WIKIPEDIA.ORG/WIKI/SANTIAGO_CALATRAVA#/MEDIA/FILE:AUDITORIO_DE_TENERIFE,_SANTA_CRUZ_DE_TENERIFE,_ESPA%C3%B1A,_2012-12-15,_DD_02.JPG **P.004**

FIGURE2: HTTPS://COMMONS.WIKIMEDIA.ORG/WIKI/FILE:ANTWERP_PORT_HOUSE_(34728338842).JPG **P.004**

FIGURE3: HTTPS://COMMONS.WIKIMEDIA.ORG/WIKI/FILE:PALAZZO_RUCELLAI,_FLORENCIA,_ITALIA,_2019_01.JPG **P.020**

FIGURE4(DORICORDER):HTTPS://COMMONS.WIKIMEDIA.ORG/WIKI/FILE:DORIC_ORDER_FROM_ATHENS_MET_DP827638.JPG **P.024**

FIGURE4 (IONIC ORDER): HTTPS://COMMONS.WIKIMEDIA.ORG/WIKI/FILE:GIOVANNI_BATTISTA_BORRA_-_REMAINS_OF_AN_IONIC_ORDER_AND_CIRCUS_AT_APHRODISIAS_-_B1977.14.948_-_YALE_CENTER_FOR_BRITISH_ART.JPG **P.024**

FIGURE5: HTTPS://COMMONS.WIKIMEDIA.ORG/WIKI/FILE:COLUMNS_IN_ST._PETER%27S_SQUARE_-_PANORAMIO.JPG **P.025**

FIGURE6: HTTPS://COMMONS.WIKIMEDIA.ORG/WIKI/FILE:DRAUGHTSMAN_MAKING_A_PERSPECTIVE_DRAWING_OF_A_RECLINING_WOMAN_MET_DT248024.JPG **P.034**

FIGURE7: HTTPS://COMMONS.WIKIMEDIA.ORG/WIKI/FILE:PROSPETTIVA3D_6.PNG **P.034**

FIGURE8:HTTPS://UPLOAD.WIKIMEDIA.ORG/WIKIPEDIA/COMMONS/9/9F/ICHNOGRAPHIAM_CAMPI_MARTII_ANTIQUAE_URBIS.JPG **P.037**

FIGURE9: PHOTO OF TOWARDS AN ARCHITECTURE, TAKEN BY THE AUTHOR **P.045**

FIGURE10: UNIDENTIFIED ARTIST; WALTER GROPIUS, PREFABRICATED COPPER HOUSES, 1931-1932: CONSTRUCTION, HARVARD ART MUSEUMS/BUSCH-REISINGER MUSEUM, GIFT OF WALTER GROPIUS, PHOTO © PRESIDENT AND FELLOWS OF HARVARD COLLEGE, BRGA.57.249.B **P.046**

FIGURE11:HTTPS://COMMONS.WIKIMEDIA.ORG/WIKI/FILE:LLOYDS_OF_LONDON_BUILDING_(DEC_2014).JPG**P.053**

FIGURE12: ILLUSTRATION REPRODUCED BY THE AUTHOR **P.063**

FIGURE13: ILLUSTRATION REPRODUCED BY THE AUTHOR **P.070**

FIGURE14: ILLUSTRATION REPRODUCED BY THE AUTHOR **P.071**

FIGURE15: ILLUSTRATION REPRODUCED BY THE AUTHOR **P.071**

FIGURE16: HTTPS://COMMONS.WIKIMEDIA.ORG/WIKI/FILE:TIMGAD_-_EXPANSION_IN_2ND_AND_3RD_CENTURY.JPG **P.075**

FIGURE17: HTTPS://COMMONS.WIKIMEDIA.ORG/WIKI/FILE:%EC%84%9C%EC%9A%B8_%ED%95%9C%EA%B0%95%EB%B3%80%EC%9D%98_%EC%95%84%ED%8C%8C%ED%8A%B8_%EB%8B%A8%EC%A7%80.JPG **P.078**

FIGURE18: HTTPS://COMMONS.WIKIMEDIA.ORG/WIKI/FILE:EU-EE-TALLINN-LAS-LAAGNA-KOORTI.JPG **P.079**

FIGURE19:HTTPS://COMMONS.WIKIMEDIA.ORG/WIKI/FILE:ANTIQUE_URBIS_ROMAE_IMAGO..._-_DESCRIPTA_A_PYRRHO_LIGORIO..._-_BTV1B84586445.JPG **P.089**

FIGURE20: PHOTO OF COMPLEXITY AND CONTRADICTION IN ARCHITECTURE TAKEN BY THE AUTHOR **P.091**

FIGURE21: PHOTO OF COMPLEXITY AND CONTRADICTION IN ARCHITECTURE TAKEN BY THE AUTHOR **P.091**

ORO Editions
Publishers of Architecture, Art, and Design
Gordon Goff: Publisher

www.oroeditions.com
info@oroeditions.com

Published by ORO Editions

Author: Sunwoo Kim
Book Design: LoloDesign
Project Manager: Jake Anderson

10 9 8 7 6 5 4 3 2 1 First Edition

ISBN: 978-1-961856-97-4

Prepress and Print work by ORO Editions Inc.
Printed in China

ORO Editions makes a continuous effort to minimize the overall carbon footprint of its publications. As part of this goal, ORO, in association with Global ReLeaf, arranges to plant trees to replace those used in the manufacturing of the paper produced for its books. Global ReLeaf is an international campaign run by American Forests, one of the world's oldest nonprofit conservation organizations. Global ReLeaf is American Forests' education and action program that helps individuals, organizations, agencies, and corporations improve the local and global environment by planting and caring for trees.